Presented to:

_____

By:

_____

Date:

_____

Hearing God's Voice:
31 Ways God Has Been Trying To Talk To You

DR. DANIEL HAUPT AND DOROTHY DANIEL

"The one who does not expect God to speak will discount every single time when God does speak."
A.W. Tozer

ISBN: 978-1-7342003-1-7

Published by Danmil Publishing

12650 W. 64th Avenue

Arvada, CO 80004

www.danmilgroup.com

Printed in the United States of America

DEDICATIONS

Since this book is written to empower both seasoned and younger generations of leaders, I dedicate it to my Mom and Dad, Velester Gore Haupt and Rev. Dr. Rubin Haupt. At the time of this publication, they are nonagenarians, 94 and 97 years old. They have had a great journey of hearing, seeing, and sensing God's words for over nine decades.

During the 1950s, they were part of the largest migration in U.S. History; Black people who were led from the South to the North by God with their faith, strength, music, and food. They had a feeling or leading by God that today would be recognized as hearing God's voice. Thanks, Mom and Dad, for the 31 ways I often watched you respond to God's voice in leading our family into change that was necessary to give us the win for our destiny. Your love, wisdom, guidance, and patience will not be forgotten.

Also, I dedicate this work to the 97 percent who are wandering generalities; those who are not yet the 3 percent who are destiny specific. I pray this book will activate you to discern God's purpose for you by hearing His Voice.

Dr. Daniel Haupt
destinycommunitycenter.org
voiceofdestiny.org

Realizing I have come this far by faith and that faith has allowed me to hear the voice of God. Communing with God's Spirit has persuaded me to co-author this book, which I dedicate to my ever-supportive husband, Edmund Daniel Sr. I know God has been speaking to you, also; and to our amazing sons and their wives, Edmund II (Chantel) and Carlos (Eva). Carlos and Eva, thank you so much for going the extra mile every day. I love you all so much.

To all of my friends and family members, thank you, for allowing me to hone the gifts that God has so graciously given me with patience and love, without judgement.

Prophet Dorothy Daniel
The Gift of Love Ministry
Tgolm.net

WHAT LEADERS ARE SAYING ABOUT THIS BOOK

As a true example of modern-day prophets, Dr. Daniel Haupt and Dorothy Daniel, both possess the gift of prophecy and writes out of their experiences and unique ability to clearly and accurately discern God's voice. In their book, *Hearing God's Voice: 31 Ways God Has Been Trying to Talk to You,* the authors address the important truth that God still speaks, then enumerates the various means through which God speaks today. This is a biblical and practical work, designed to empower the reader to tune into the mind of God and begin the process of hearing His voice. This series of engaging conversations is a must read for anyone desiring a more intimate and personal encounter with the voice of our Creator.

> Felix Gilbert, D. Min.
> Director Urban Initiatives
> & Assistant Professor of Pastoral Ministry
> Denver Seminary
> Denver, CO

Hearing God's Voice has been published at a time when the popular opinion seems to outweigh both the written and spoken Word of God. With busy lifestyles, routines, and family obligations, many are skeptical as to whether God still speaks and if so, what He is saying? In this book, the authors confirm that not only is He speaking, but He speaks in at least 31 ways. *Hearing God's Voice* takes the guesswork out of hearing from God and teaches the reader, using easy to understand lessons and exercises, to hear from God for themselves. The authors simply, yet, significantly, move our hearts to tune into His voice. Expect great moves of God as you read and apply what you learn here. In other words, read it and reap!"

Dr. Katrina Ferguson
CEO of the Ultimate Coaching Exchange,
Best-Selling Author, Speaker and Entrepreneur

Simply amazing! This book gives all who read it a new hope of hearing the voice of God with clarity. I believe many will have a God encounter as they read through the pages.

Pastor Randy Lucero
Word Alive Church

"Hearing God's Voice: 31 Ways God Has Been Trying To Talk To You" is life-changing book. Together, co-authors Dr. Daniel Haupt and Prophet Dorothy Daniel open the eyes of our hearts to the reality that God truly desires to communicate with us.

In reading this book, I sensed the sincere heart of the authors as they took the *cliché* off the frequently used words, "God loves you" and presented the diverse ways He loves us. Their writings are an undeniable witness of His true, passionate, and relentless love for us. The authors reveal the many ways God seeks to show how He longs for us to hear Him for our own lives, and to speak to others through the gifting He has given. They carefully unfold His great longing for you to be a co-creator and co-worker with Him as they strategically put together *31 ways He's trying to communicate to you.*

Hearing God's Voice carries a frequency to energize you to deepen your walk with God, to hear God and to share words of edification, exhortation, and comfort to others.

Apostle Jimmie Reed
Founder, Global Manifestations

First of all, I appreciate the authors of this book, Dr. Daniel Haupt and Prophet Dorothy Daniel, for putting their hard-working efforts into this most-needed book. *Hearing God's Voice* can help readers understand that God Almighty truly loves His creation and wants to communicate with us.

Through biblical examples, they expose the deep understanding that God is unlimited, and He has many communicating channels through which He talks to His creation. *Hearing God's Voice* provides the knowledge to enable God's people to recognize and discern the many ways He speaks. Thus, this work can help one experience a closer relationship with God.

Indeed, this book reads like an "Inspirational Chat" on listening to the voice of God and missing nothing that is coming directly from the authors' hearts. It provides opportunity for the hearts of all who desire to have a more intimate relationship with God Almighty. This book should be read by every believer.

> Shaw K. Barkat
> International Evangelist
> Director/ President
> Nation Builders International
> Community Development Center Inc.

Hearing God's Voice lays out an easy to understand process for a closer connection with God. The authors, Dr. Daniel Haupt and Prophet Dorothy Daniel, have provided this timely and relevant resource. This book is a must read for anyone who desires to discern and clearly hear God's voice.

> Dr. Derrick E. Haynes, President
> CEO, Your Career Doctor

TABLE OF CONTENTS

Chapter Eight

Chapter Nine

Chapter Ten

Chapter Eleven

Chapter Thirteen

Chapter Fourteen

Chapter Fifteen

Chapter Sixteen

Chapter Seventeen

Chapter Eighteen

INTRODUCTION

B race yourself for a spiritual and learning experience with unlimited possibilities as you read *"Hearing God's Voice: 31 Ways God Has Been Trying to Talk to You."* The pages ahead are an "outside-of-the-box" revelation for hearing God's voice in familiar and unfamiliar ways. Authors, Dr. Daniel Haupt and Prophet Dorothy Daniel, have created a unique work to acquaint readers with the many channels through which God speaks to us.

The content is comprised of an entrée of delectable chapters and channels to indulge you in the partaking of its fruitful offerings. This book contains interesting topics, including: "Why God Wants to Speak to Us Today," "God Speaks to Clarify Purposes…," "God Speaks to Download Safety and Protection," and "Understanding Channels and Methods For Hearing God's Voice." Also, you can explore many channels through which God speaks: Scripture, Prayer and Fasting, Meditations, Silence, Journaling, Word of Knowledge, Word of Wisdom, Dreams, Visions, Prophecy, Encounters and Visitations, Signs and Wonders, Government and Authorities, Artistic Expressions, and more.

The authors prayerfully designed this work to provoke thinking, stir the spirit, and break down barriers of communication between God and people. As emphasized throughout this book, every person can learn how to hear what God is saying to him or her. Once distraction, static, distortion, and confusion are removed, an understanding of how to tune in to God's communication channels can be established. Then, a clear divine connection is accessible. These inhibiting and deafening issues are dealt with, so that readers may overcome whatever prevents them from hearing God's voice.

This is a progressive and equipping book, providing a critical solution—how to hear God's voice and obeying Him during these perilous times. When hearing from or being inspired by God, right choices become clearer. Today, deciding whether to take a vaccine, board a particular plane, travel a different root home, or grocery shop another day, can be the difference between life and death. Sometime God tells us to reach out and help a neighbor, relative, co-worker, friend, or stranger because He wants to bless the receiver and giver beyond expectations. So, the knowledge offered within the forthcoming chapters, probably means more than can be determined now. Therefore, reading and studying this book can further equip you for current and future end-time victorious living.

Minister Ella Coleman
Publisher, Life & Book Consultant/Coach
Ellavation Publishing, LLC
Purpose For Life Foundation

CHAPTER ONE
THE GOD WHO TALKS

How precious also are Your thoughts to me, O God! How great is the sum of them! If I should count them, they would be more in number than the sand; when I awake, I am still with You.
Psalm 139:17-18 NKJV

There is only one supreme and living God who has made Himself known throughout the ages. He is God, the Creator, Maker and Sustainer of the universe. Yet, the world has not known this true and living God. Instead, because of sin they have remained alienated from God. Consequently, people have created many idols since the dawn of time. Idolatrous concepts furnished through religions and human philosophies are enshrouded with different superstitious doctrines. Idols are carved out of wood or made from metals and precious stones, but the living God is the uncreated Creator of life and the ultimate source of all existence. We serve the God who has sustained the universe by His power and designed everything that ever came to be.

This same sovereign God has maintained an unbroken communion and connection with His most esteemed creation (man and woman) from the very beginning. The first chapter of the Bible, Genesis 1, reveals that Elohim (one of His names) is a God who talks. From the beginning of creation, the earth was dark, formless, empty, and void. The Spirit of the Lord hovered on the surface of the deep. Then, in Genesis 1:2, "God said, 'Let there be light' and there was light." God spoke light and life into being and the rich beautiful earth was formed. At that point, He revealed Himself as the God who speaks and performs actions with words. On the sixth day, He had completed our complex universe, installed the sun and moon into place, apportioned the boundaries of the sea, and made the earth dry land, inhabitable for life to thrive on.

He does not reveal Himself as an influence or a mystical force in space. Even though He is shrouded in mystery, He has never ceased to seek fellowship with us, for we are created in His image and fashioned after His likeness. This means just like God is a Spirit, we are spirits, although in human bodies.

Moreover, God desired more than just plants, fish, birds, insects, cattle, and other animals on earth. He desired friends with whom He could fellowship; intelligent beings, indigenes earth dwellers; people capable of communing with Him and establishing His counsel. God desired people on this planet He could talk to; governors of the created realm who would take direct orders from Him and implement them in the new world; beings capable of developing linguistic systems of communication. Beyond the biological process of reproduction seen in other animals, humans have spirit and soul to establish connection with God. It was intentional by God that we are modeled after the likeness of His divinity.

GOD SPOKE FROM HIS DIVINITY AT THE BEGINNING

*"Then God said, **Let us** make man in Our image, according to Our likeness; let them have dominion over the fish of the sea, over the birds, over the cattle, over all the earth and over every creeping thing that creeps on earth. So God created man in His own image; in the image of God He created him; male and female He created them."*
Genesis 1: 26-27 NKJV

"Let us" in the scripture above means God was not alone at creation. The Godhead—Father, Son, and Holy Spirit—maintain an eternally unbroken communication that makes them one in three persons. That is, the same God in three persons. He came as the Son, yet He is still the God of heaven and earth. Now we have Him with us as the Holy Spirit, and He remains God.

There is also communication among the angels. Angels like Gabriel, the messenger and Michael, the warrior, are among other angelic beings who carryout assignments from God and worship Him faithfully. On the other hand, Lucifer, once the most glorious angel, defected wickedly and was able to win one third of the angels against God in the war in Heaven (Revelation 12: 7-12). Then, of course, the wicked angels, (now demons) were kicked out of Heaven. But what is revealed from both good and evil angels is that God relates and speaks to His created beings and bestows rewards or judgements accordingly.

Our primary focus in this book is to reveal how God speaks to *us* because we ought to know that our Creator is a God who speaks. He communicates in heaven and on earth through many channels, which will be covered in this book.

GOD SPOKE TO ADAM AND EVE

(Genesis 3:9–19)

Adam and Eve, the progenitors of the human race, were not only created to govern and have dominion on earth, but for fellowship with God. We are not designed to walk the length of our days without God! Sadly, from the first-time man disobeyed God, his heart has been disconnected from God. A disconnected life from God involves a lot of struggles, destiny becomes a promise with doubt, and the future is bleak and gloom with many uncertainties. Communication with God was crucial at creation and the disconnection caused by their sin was devastating for Adam and Eve.

We love to imagine how perfect and beautiful Eden was. The flourishing fountains, clean rivers, green hills, rich garden, blissful climate, friendly animals, perfect relationships, which makes our souls long for the rediscovery of this lost paradise. The presence of God envelops that world and as we find out in Genesis 3: 8-9, God would sometimes come down in person to build community with Adam and Eve. He walks among trees, calls them by their names and cultivates friendship with them. Adam and Eve could hear and respond to God's voice. Their ears were opened, their hearts were connected, and their eyes could see the magnificence of the King of heaven and all creation. God made it clear, the earth was created for them (Adam and Eve) and they were to tend and keep it healthy. They received direct instructions from God; no medium, no prophets, no psychics, and no oracles mediated between them.

The Serpent acknowledged this when he asked Eve if God had said anything to them. Eve confirmed that in one of their conversations, God instructed them not to eat of the tree of knowledge of good and evil. Adam and Eve heard God clearly; they understood Him and knew His voice. No wonder they went into hiding when God called out to them after they had eaten of the forbidden tree. When God called, they could differentiate His voice from every other voice. But their disobedience had caused total trust and openness with God to turn into mistrust and shame; not because God had changed but due to their own fall from innocence and purity to guilt and impurity. Unfortunately, they could not regain their original state, nor could the rest of the human family that has followed.

GOD SPOKE TO AND THROUGH ENTITIES

Several scriptures reveal that there are times God speaks *to* and *through* other entities like animals and trees. He spoke directly to the serpent in Genesis 3:14-15. *"And the LORD God said unto the serpent, Because thou hast done this, thou art cursed above all cattle, and above every beast of the field; upon thy belly shalt eat dust all the days of your life."* Also, we read in Mark 11:12-14 how Jesus spoke directly to the fig tree.

The next day as they were leaving Bethany, Jesus was hungry. Seeing in the distance a fig tree in leaf, he went to find out if it had any fruit. When he reached it, he found nothing but leaves, because it was not the season for figs. Then he said to the tree, "May no one ever eat fruit from you again." And his disciples heard him say it.

Also, there are other entities God speaks through. For example, in Genesis 3, while Moses led his father-in-law's flock on Mount Horeb, he noticed a burning bush in flames but unconsumed. When he turned to observe the mystery, God spoke to him. At another instance in Numbers 22:27, Prophet Balaam had been summoned by Balak to curse the people of Israel and God did not want him to go. However, since the offer was tempting and the call was persistent, he decided to go without the approval of God. *"So, Balaam rose in the morning, saddled his donkey, and went with the princes of Moab. Then God's anger was aroused because he went, and the Angel of the Lord took His stand in the way as an adversary against him. And he was riding upon his donkey, and his two servants were with him. Now the donkey saw the Angel of the Lord standing in the way with His drawn sword in his hand, and the donkey turned aside out of the way and went into the field. So, Balaam struck the donkey to turn her back onto*

the road. Then the Angel of the Lord stood in a narrow path between the vineyards, with a wall on this side and a wall on that side. And when the donkey saw the Angel of the Lord, she pushed herself against the wall and crushed Balaam's foot against the wall; so he stuck her again. Then the Lord opened the mouth of the donkey, and she said unto Balaam, 'What have I done to you, that you have stuck me these three times?' And Balaam said unto the donkey, 'Because you have abused me. I wish there were a sword in my hand, for now would I kill you!' And the donkey said unto Balaam, 'Am not I your donkey on which you have ridden ever since I became yours?'"
Numbers 22: 21-30 NKJV

GOD SPEAKS TO PEOPLE FROM ALL WALKS OF LIFE

Adam and Eve were not the only humans God spoke to. The Bible is full of accounts of prophets, kings, leaders, warriors, and everyday people, who encountered and experienced relationship with God. God spoke with Cain (Genesis 4:9–15); Noah (Genesis 6:13, Genesis 7:1, Genesis 8:15) and his sons (Genesis 9:1-8); and with Abraham and his wife Sarah (Genesis 18). It is written in Exodus 33: 11 that "the LORD spoke to Moses face to face, as a man speaks to his friend." God confirms this in Numbers 12: 8 when He says, "I speak with him [Moses] face to face, clearly and not in riddles." Enoch's fellowship was so intense with God that God took him out of the world alive (Genesis 5: 21-24). The Bible is surely the sacred message of God that reveals how God had connected with humans from the beginning and clarifies how God still talks to them today.

We are glad to inform you that God also wants to speak to you as His child and friend today. In spite of heaven being light years from earth, God has developed unique technologies and channels through which He can maintain constant connection with us. We are the sheep of His flock and we know the voice of our Master. There are communication systems established through which humanity can engage divinity. We can tap into His thoughts and hear what He is saying without the interruption of time. God speaks through mental and visual images, physical and heartfelt sensation, and through the vehicle of words audible and inaudible voices.

Like tuning into a radio station is required to receive the signal from the channel, we must learn to align with the frequency of heaven, in order to hear God speak to us. The primary element necessary in conversing with God is faith. Without faith, it is impossible to please God (Hebrews 11: 6). We will identify at least 31 channels through which God speaks to us.

Do you need the divine guidance of God in the path of your destiny? Do you feel lost in the darkness in a world disconnected from God? Are you broken under the weight of despair and depression? God wants to speak life to you. He wants you to hear Him and partake of the eternal peace He has paid dearly for. There are at least 31 channels through which God speaks to us in this book and as you prayerfully engage it, we pray that you will be empowered to know your purpose and the priority of your destiny vocation. Amen.

CHAPTER TWO
WHY GOD WANTS TO SPEAK TO US TODAY

Behold, I stand at the door and knock: if any man hears my voice, and
opens the door, I will come in to him, and dine with him, and him with Me.
Revelation 3:20 NKJV

You might wonder why God is so interested in talking to you. After all, He is God, worshiped for all eternity by angelic beings. He could go on without us, but He chooses not to. We are His children; and He formed us to be like Him. His love for us is deeper than the deepest depths and as shoreless as eternity. He calls us the apple of His eyes and hides us in the shadow of His wings (Psalm 17: 8). We are so precious to Him that He gave up His throne and left His glory behind and took on the fallen form of man. The Word that called all things into being became flesh and lived among us (John 1: 14). He walked the earth preaching the love He has for humanity. Then, He went up to the cursed cross to die a cruel death for the redemption of the lost human race and the reconciliation of the world back to our Father God.

Christ paid the ultimate price when He bore our sins in His body on the cross, so that we might die to sins and live in righteousness

(1 Peter 2: 24). Prophet Isaiah captured the love of God towards us in detail when he described Christ as a man who for our sake was acquainted with grief. He was despised and rejected on His road to Calvary but gladly bore our grief and carried our sorrows. He was afflicted for our sins, wounded for our transgressions, and bruised for our iniquities. The chastisement for our peace was upon Him and by the stripes He received, we are healed (Isaiah 53). "For God so loved the world that He gave his only Son…" (John 3: 16).

You are so loved by God. His love for you is not conditional; it cannot be earned or learned (since it has no end). It is not deserved but given. No one is too lost for the loving hand of the Savior to reach and no sin is too much for the blood of the sacrificial Lamb to wash. God wants to speak to you because you are His. Satan, sin, and sickness are not your masters. You might think you have lived so much of your life without the Savior, but the truth is, even in the silence and distance, God constantly reaches out to you to make known His affection for you. He says in Jeremiah 29:11 (NIV), "For I know the plans I have for you, declares the Lord, 'plans to prosper you and not to harm you, plans to give you a hope and a future.'"

Aside from the fact that God loves us beyond words, we are created for fellowship, also. Separation from God is never part of the original design. God declared in Leviticus 26:12, "I will walk among you and be your God, and you shall be my people." Similarly, He said in Joel 2:28, "I will pour out my Spirit on all people. Your sons and daughters will prophesy, your old men will dream dreams, your young men will see visions."

Why has God given us two ears and one mouth? James 1: 19 (NIV) answers this by saying, "Everyone should be quick to listen and slow to speak." The reason why the world has continually plunged into darkness is because the hearts of many people are hardened with sin and their eyes are veiled from seeing who they truly are. We are created for more. God wants to direct our path and guide our feet each moment of the way.

God is compelled to use three **Common Methods** to build relationship, communicate instructions and give us directions. No one is created to live on the earth without guidance. Even though we all have all wandered off in sin, yet God made no drifters. We all belong to God and He wants to direct us, establish His values, and reveal His intended operation for our lives. God achieves this by speaking through these common methods:

A. Words—An Audible and Inaudible Voice.

B. Imagery—Open Vision and Inner Vision; Dreams and Trances.

C. Sensory Sensation—Physical and Heart Felt.

Although He employs these operations to talk to us, He is not limited to the mentioned three. God uses other channels in communicating His thoughts to us. We are spiritual beings living in a biological frame (body) and uniquely designed and wired to hear and capture God's voice and mind from heaven to earth. One important reason why God wants to speak to us is to nurture intimacy between Him and us. We are not toy soldiers without freewill; we are His children and friends. The Bible says, "Whether you turn to the right or to the left, your ears will hear a voice behind you, saying, this is the way walk in it" (Isaiah 30: 21).

Isaiah 48: 17 (NIV) puts it like this:

"Thus says the LORD, your Redeemer, the Holy One of Israel: 'I am the LORD your God, who teaches you for your benefit, who directs you in the way you should go.'"

Our Father and Creator knows the end from the beginning; He understands the terrains of life and the challenges of the day are not strange to Him. This is why He wants to lead you along the unknown road of life and guide you through the unfamiliar path of time. He will turn darkness into light before you and rough places into level ground. He will not leave nor forsake you. He has promised all this in Isaiah 42: 10.

The knowledge and fellowship of God is the secret to an enduring victory in life. The misery of a soul is not measured by the lack of material wealth but by the disconnection that exists between such life and God Himself. The world and her riches are both fading, the treasures of life can be stolen, burnt or destroyed but the fellowship of God will outlive the sun. Jesus was very precise by stating in Luke 12: 15 the life of a man does not consist in the abundance of the things he possesses. Regardless of your earthly assets or possessions, if you do not have an established connection with your Maker, you are a bankrupt soul. This is why it is written in Daniel 11:32 that "They that know God shall be strong and do great and mighty exploits." Everyone may be frustrated in this world of fears and crises but they that wait on God will renew their strength, they shall mount up with wings like eagles, they shall run and not be weary, they shall walk and not stumble (Isaiah 40: 31).

Do you also desire a fellowship and connection with the Redeemer of the world? How sweet and blissful is the tender voice of the Savior. He speaks strength to the weak, life to the dead, healing and recovery to the sick, growth and wisdom to His children, comfort to the troubled, encouragement to those in despair, liberty to the enslaved, faith to the fearful, hope to the hopeless and redemption to the lost. Do you also desire His voice to counsel you into the reality of your destiny and nurture you in the right path all the rest of your life? God is willing to cross the galaxies just to fellowship with you. Also, He wants to be your Father and your Friend. Only open the door of your heart to Him and He will gladly take His throne and run the course of your life.

CHAPTER THREE

GOD SPEAKS TO CHOSEN VESSELS IN SCRIPTURE, HISTORY, AND TODAY

Your ears will hear a word behind you, saying,
"This is the way, walk in it,' wherever you turn
to the right hand or whenever you turn to the left.
Isaiah 30: 21

I t is established that our God is the living and speaking God. The Bible reveals how men and women across all generations and ages have had lives built on partnerships and relationships with the Father. Adam in Eden, Cain in the field, Moses at Sinai, Elijah in the cave, Jacob at Bethel, Saul (Paul) on his way to Damascus, are just a few of the many instances of who God spoke to in the Bible. From the dawn of time and through all generations, God has never ceased to commune with His own. His ways of interacting with humans might vary from time to time and from people to people, yet, He has always made His will known to those whose ears are opened to His voice. Plus, He has always directed the feet of the righteous who have inclined their hearts to His wisdom and speak to the ears of those He was leading to repentance.

THE WOMAN AT THE WELL

He told her, "Go, call your husband and come back."
"I have no husband," she replied. Jesus said to her, "You are right when you
say you have no husband. The fact is, you had five husbands, and the man
you now have is not your husband. What you have said is quite true."
John 4:16-18 NIV

Indeed, the Samaritan woman at the well had been with five husbands in the past. Obviously, she had known many betrayals and disappointments in all her previous relationships. Her life was out of order and in a complete mess. Lost in hopelessness, she declared to the Savior, "I have no husband," even though she lived with a man. Like many people in the world today, she was already pushed to the wall of defeat with seemingly no way out.

However, when a person comes in contact with the word of God, everything can change. She heard the voice of Christ at the well of Jacob and her life was better for it. That was a woman who had been shrouded in shame and rejection most her life. She received a new life of purpose and focus as she went out into the street of Sychar with boundless joy, spreading the good tidings of a Hebrew man who had shown her all she had done.

The voice of the Creator brings all things into divine alignment; it sets purpose in place and gives meaning to the formless voids of lives. Just as she was transformed by the voice of the King, there is no human life too ruined to be healed or too lost to be restored.

GOD SPEAKS TO PEOPLE, EFFECTING CHANGE AND RELEASING POWER TO ACT ON HIS VISION.

For the word of God is quick, and powerful, and sharper than any two-edged sword, piercing even to the dividing asunder of soul and spirit, and of the joints and marrow, and is a discerner of the thoughts and intents of the heart.
Hebrews 4: 12 KJV

Clearly, from the story of this Samaritan woman, God speaks to effect change and release power to act on His vision. He is specific in His interaction and purposeful in His engagements. His word is quick, powerful, and sharper than the sword. Notorious Saul heard the master's voice on Damascus Road to persecute the Christians. This encounter did not only knock him off his horse but knocked out the self-righteous wickedness in him and transformed him to Paul, a man completely empowered for a new and glorious destiny. There are so many Sauls today who only need to hear the tender voice of their Maker. There are so many like the woman of Samaria, who only need to experience or encounter Jesus in order to move away from the enslaving zones of depression and confusion, and walk into the newness of life purchased by Christ on the cross for the world.

GOD CLARIFIES PURPOSES AND DISTINGUISHES BETWEEN SACRED AND COMMON

The entrance of thy word giveth light, it giveth understanding unto the simple.
Psalm 119: 130 KJV

The word of God comes to us to also enlighten us about the mysteries and hidden things of the kingdom. As God's oracles, we have access to the wisdom that sustains the universe. Because of our connection to heaven, we have the grace to walk through life with unmatched wisdom. Daniel, for example, was ten times better than his contemporaries in Babylon. Similarly, there was no one regarded as wise as Joseph in the entire nation of Egypt.

When confused about what career path to follow, turn to God for direction. God also speaks to clarify purposes. You are not meant to be in the dark about the reason why you were born. God wants to reveal your purpose, show, and guide you along the route to your other side of through, a place of divine destiny. He will help you to distinguish between that which is sacred and that which is not.

GOD SPEAKS TO DOWNLOAD SAFETY AND PROTECTION

Life is full of many uncertainties and because we do not know what the future holds, many of us live in perpetual fear and anxiety of what tomorrow may bring. Troubled by the unknown, we can easily slip into doubt and wonder if our dreams will ever be fulfilled. Yet, no need to worry. There is an absolute peace that comes with hearing God through at least 31 of His channels. He speaks to protect and direct us in the path of safety. Insist on taking time for prayer and meditation to hear, see, and sense God's voice behind you saying the equivalent of, "This is the way, walk in it." Communicating with God keeps you "under the shadow of the Almighty" as stated in Psalms 91:1. God speaks to download safety and protection to us.

CHAPTER FOUR
WIRED FOR DIVINE COMMUNICATION

G od has wired us to be His prophetic radio operators and communication officers. He wants to reach the world through us and until we are connected in communication with unbroken access to the heart of God, the world will continually wait in vain for answers. The creation waits eagerly for the manifestation of the children of God (Romans 8: 19). The world needs you to be connected to your Heavenly Father, so that you may bring direction to a directionless world, life to a dying people, and meaning to a confused generation.

Yes, you are uniquely created and called for divine communication. However, our personalities, individual frames and make-ups all determine and shape how God chooses to speak and communicate to each of us in conversation. God speaks to each of us individually; your culture, nature, experiences, worldviews, temperament, influence how we perceive God, interpret His heart, and apply it to our situation. An introvert is likely to hear God through different channels and experience divine communication differently than an extrovert. A left-brain oriented person would likely process divine information differently when compared to a right-brain person. Understanding your personality is key to identifying the channels through which God speaks to you. Personality gives us a unique lens through which we see the world. It serves as a pattern, predicator or model for life and greatly influences what we are and what we will become. David Funder defines personality as "a collection of relatively discrete, independent and narrow social capacities." It involves your character, temperament, disposition, worldview, and other traits. The way God has made you (personality) was determined by what He desires you to become.

LEFT-BRAIN AND RIGHT-BRAIN ORIENTATION

The brain is a vital organ containing about 100 billion neurons and 100 trillion connections. The brain controls everything you do, think, and feel. It is divided into two hemispheres with specialized functions. As scientists continue to map the brain, we are gaining more insight on how the brain works.

It is believed that people are either left-brained or right-brained. This means that for everyone, one part of the brain is dominant. For instance, if you are usually very analytical and methodical in your thinking, such as Luke in the Bible, you are left-brain oriented. Some of the characteristics of a left-brained person include but are not limited to linear thinking, fact computations, logic, writing and reading. The Old Testament scribe and book, Ezra, is another left-brain example. On the other hand, if you are more creative or artistic, you are believed to be right-brained such as King Solomon. A right-brained person is more artistic. Some of the traits of these people include holistic thinking, imagination, artistry, rhythm, music, dance, and intuition. Moses' sister, Miriam, was probably right brained.

These characteristics affect the channels through which God speaks to us. There are people who discover mysteries of God out of careful and detailed research and reading. They compare scriptures and Bible versions, retrieve, and connect ancient records, analyze historical and religious documents, uncovering the mysteries and truth of God. While another who is right-brained oriented might just sit with a verse as God inspires his or her intuitively to discover hidden meanings of the engrafted word. In which category do you belong? It is important to understand your personality to know which way you are wired to receive words and directions from God.

PERSONALITY: INTROVERTS AND EXTROVERTS

Another aspect of personality is the social disposition one has developed over time. An individual's social personality is usually between being an introvert, extrovert, or a blend of the two. This was first proposed in the 1960s when psychologist Carl Jung recognized these two identifiable social traits. An introvert is a reserved and thoughtful individual who does not seek out special attention or social engagement. They feel uncomfortable being in the spotlight, leading a conversation or being central to a public activity. They get exhausted and drained with continuous interaction, and they simply enjoy their own company. They enjoy being alone. An extrovert is directly opposite of an introvert. Extroverts are people who love conversations, social gatherings, public interaction, parties, and a busy environment. They are bored with loneliness and cannot cope with constraints or silence. They love to talk. Others may never be able to keep calm or get bored around them.

You are probably an introvert if you prefer a lot of time alone. Being home alone is thrilling for some while it could be the greatest punishment for others. There are people who love solitude. In fact, silence is crucial to their happiness. They use such time to write, read, watch movies, and so on. Even at work, they prefer to be alone. Isolation allows introverts to focus deeply and produce high quality work. When they are compelled or obligated to work with others, they simply avoid the social aspect and focus on doing what is required. An extrovert loves company. They are very lively and vocal.

Both personalities are crucial to how God relates with each of us. Introverts have an active inner thought process that leads them toward self-reflection and research. You are more of an introverted person if you are more comfortable writing out your thoughts rather than speaking them. This is especially true when you are unprepared, or you prefer to think through your response because your communication style is focused and considerate. Because an introverted person is usually quiet and intuitive, do not be surprised if God speaks to you through the inner or still small voice of the Holy Spirit. As an introvert, you are likely to be more emotionally sensitive and God can connect with you through the sensation channel. This also includes the intrinsic interpretation of models, natural phenomenon, and kinetic demonstration of hands. For an extrovert person, God can speak to you through people, the word, divine visitation, and other socially inclined means.

Nevertheless, most people are not purely introverted or purely extroverted. They fall somewhere in the middle having both characteristics. Some characteristics may be stronger and our God who understands the absolute frame of all His children will choose how best to relate with each of us.

CULTURAL, EXPERIENTIAL, AND DESTINY MODEL

About noon the following day as they were on their journey and approaching the city, Peter went up on the roof to pray. He became hungry and wanted something to eat and while the meal was being prepared, he fell into a trance. He saw heaven opened and something like a large sheet with four corners being let down to earth. It contained all kinds of four-footed animals, as well as reptiles and birds. Then a voice told him, "Get up, Peter. Kill and eat." "Surely not, Lord!" Peter replied. "I have never eaten anything impure or unclean." The voice spoke to him a second time, "Do not call anything impure that God has made clean." This happened three times, and immediately the sheet was taken back to heaven.
Acts 10:9-16

This scriptural account of Peter's cultural-specific reaction to what God told him to do in the trace, would have been the typical response of most Jews during that time. Eating unclean animals was unacceptable. The law of Moses was clear about what creatures

Hebrews could and could not eat, so Peter responded accordingly. Because the message in the trace was referring to the acceptance of salvation for the Gentiles, it was necessary that God communicate it three times to Peter. This example shows how culture has a great role to play in the determination of our personalities, particularly how we respond to situations.

Culture introduces the shared values, including beliefs and how people think, feel, or even act. Culture describes the way we learn, live, believe, and behave. It is a way of life, including ideology, customs, traditions, and the social behavior of a particular person, ethnic group, nation, or society. The value system and world view of people affect the way they see people, environments, and situations. Like we notice in the case of Peter, our culture and social ideology has a role to play in our communication with God. God used things considered an abomination in Peter's culture to teach him that the salvation of God is not only for the Jews but the whole world. He would not touch the spread sheet of meals from heaven because it had reptiles and four legged animals which are forbidden in the Mosaic tradition. Cornelius, a gentile, was a good man who had encountered God in his closet through the visitation of angels, but he needed an apostle to pray for him and guide him into deeper understanding of Christ (Acts 10). Peter was the right man for this assignment and God came culturally to inform him not to discriminate against anyone. Our culture can influence how God communicates with us.

Similarly, past experiences have an impact on who we become and how we view life. Consequently, this influences the channel of divine communication for everyone. How we view our past experiences both consciously and subconsciously shape how we approach life. Our past is ingrained in us. Humans are a habitual species, so what we do every day becomes like an automatic program, which affects how we approach situations. Our personalities and how God intricately wired us to tune into His mind set and capture his voice, will determine which channel He chooses to communicate with us.

CHAPTER FIVE

HEARING GOD'S VOICE AT EVERY LEVEL OF FAITH

The voice of God is not exclusive for those with a certain level of spiritual maturity. It is not a luxury for the oldest Christians. As the air is crucial to the survival of the infant, youth, young adult, and aged, so is the word of God to everyone in the fold of faith. God demonstrated this by speaking to people of different ages, spiritual stature, and social status. He spoke to Hagar (whose faith had no depth in the knowledge of the God of her master, Abraham) at the spring in the desert (Genesis 16:7). He spoke to Pharaoh (a gentle king of Egypt) through dreams (Genesis 41). He spoke to the little boy, Samuel, who was so naïve to recognize or differentiate the voice of God from humans (1 Samuel 3) and He spoke Saul on his way to Damascus to persecute the Church (Acts 9:1-19).

Many think their inability to hear from God is because they are not like a prophet, pastor, or spiritually high enough. The Scriptures and the story model in the Bible dispel this false theory. Do you remember that God spoke to the Serpent in the Garden? Even though Pharaoh had a hardened heart, God still spoke to him. He spoke to Joseph and Samuel when they were yet children. This reveals that you do not need to become a bishop or an apostle before you can hear God. If unbelievers can hear God and sometimes get directives from him like the case of Pharaoh and if animals can hear the voice of God like the case of Balaam's donkey and the serpent at Eden, how much more you, who is redeemed to be His own child. Job 35:11 (NKJV) spells it out that God is the one "Who teaches us more than the beasts of the earth and makes us wiser than the birds of heaven."

We are created in His image and the worst of us all are still reachable with the voice of the Maker. He speaks to the heart of the sinner and convicts him of his sins until he repents. He also gives the youth the reassuring whisper that He has taken care of the future. He breaths peace into the heart of the elders and strength into the bones of the young. He speaks to us many times in different ways, but like the boy Samuel in the Bible, we really have to learn to discern the voice of God. Samuel must have thought he was too young and inexperienced to hear from God like most of us today. Perhaps, to the young Samuel, God would have rather spoken to Eli, not him. But the word of God is not selective. He guides us through the long walk of earth and occasionally comes to point us the right way towards our destinies. You can hear God irrespective of how long or how matured you are in the faith.

Have you not read in Job 32: 8-9 (NIV) that it is not only the old who are wise and not only the aged who understands what is right? "There is a Spirit in man, and the breath of the Almighty gives him understanding." There is a Spirit in man that recognizes God's flow and inspiration in motion. God speaks to sinners and saints but often His words are not recognized because of the sinner's dull spiritual senses. Job 33:16 also says that God "opens the ears of men and seals their instruction."

Jesus illustrated this through the Parable of the Sower in Luke 8: 5-8 (NKJV).

"A sower went out to sow his seed. And as he sowed, some fell by the wayside; and it was trampled down, and the birds of the air devoured it. Some fell on rock; and as soon as it sprang up, it withered away because it lacked moisture. And some fell among thorns, and the thorns sprang up with it and choked it.

But others fell on good ground, sprang up, and yielded a crop a hundredfold." Jesus further explains this parable in verse 11-15 by saying, *"The seed is the word of God. Those by the wayside are the ones who hear; then the devil comes and takes away the word out of their hearts, lest they should believe and be saved. But the ones on the rock are those whom when they hear, receive the word with joy; and these have no root, who believe for a while and in time of temptation fall away. Now the ones who fell among thorns are those who, when they have heard, go out and are chocked with cares, riches, and pleasures of life, and bring no fruit to maturity. But the ones that fell on good ground are those who, having heard the word with a noble and good heart, keep it and bear fruit with patience."*

The word of God comes to all, but we must give it a fertile ground to grow and become productive. The parable of the sower reveals that it is possible to receive the word of God and still remain the same with no result to show for it. This explains why spiritual growth can be slow and the labor of maturity fruitless. If our hearts are not fertile and conditioned to receive the word of God and apply it to our lives, possibly it becomes ineffective in us. Beloved, hearing God's voice is experienced at every spectrum of faith but grows through consistency, quality, and quantity. Romans 10:17 (NKJV) says, "Faith comes by hearing, and hearing by the word of God."

God speaks to us to build our faith and capacity to hear and understand what He means by what He says. Hearing is an ongoing process until Rhema, Logos, and Dabar are achieved. You cannot outgrow hearing from God and there is no level of the faith that you may attain where the word of God becomes unnecessary. As Apostle Paul points out in Colossians 3:16, the word of God must dwell within you richly as you teach and admonish one another with all wisdom, and as you sing psalms, hymns, and spiritual songs with gratitude in your hearts to God.

HEARING GOD'S VOICE: A PROCESS, NOT A SINGULAR EVENT

Hearing the voice of God and tuning into His mind is not a singular event but an ongoing process of hearing, sensing, tuning, and capturing. It is not an event, but a life knitted into the very being of our spirituality. The moment you kneel in repentance at the foot of the cross, a process of connecting with God is initiated which will continue for all eternity. God wants to speak to you not just once but continuously. Hearing God's voice is a process; it takes consistency and continuity to become clearer and more audible. The story of the boy Samuel illustrates this process.

"The boy Samuel ministered before the Lord under Eli. In those days, the word of the LORD was rare; there were not many visions. One night, Eli, whose eyes were becoming so weak that he could barely see, was lying down in his usual place. The Lamp of God had not yet gone out, and Samuel was lying down in the temple of the LORD, where the ark of God was. Then the Lord called Samuel. Samuel answered, 'Here I am.' And he ran to Eli and said, 'Here I am; you called me.' But Eli said, 'I did not call; go back and lie down.' So, he went and lay down. Again, the LORD called, 'Samuel!' And Samuel got up and went to Eli and said, 'Here I am; you called me.' 'My son,' Eli said, 'I did not call; go back and lie down.' **Now Samuel did not yet know the LORD: The word of the LORD had not yet been revealed to him.** *The LORD called Samuel a third time, and Samuel got up and went to Eli and said, 'Here I am; you called me.' Then Eli realized that the LORD was calling the boy. So Eli told Samuel, "Go and lie down, and if He calls you, say, 'Speak, for your servant is listening"'* (1 Samuel 3:1-10).

Samuel's first encounter with God reflects how many of us were at the very beginning of our relationship with God. It is normal to initially struggle in recognizing or differentiating the voice of God. There are times we wonder if it is really God talking or just our feelings or hearts trying to play God. Can you imagine, the great Prophet Samuel once struggled to hear God. Do not be discouraged when you are still finding it hard to correctly discern the voice of God as well. Learning to hear the Voice of God and capture his mind or intelligence is often a process of human activation. You have to be deliberate about aligning, verifying and responding when you hear God's voice. You must be ready to patiently wait to receive from God. The Old Testament School of the Prophets was a forerunner of prophetic activation that has its application in the work of the new testament prophet. It is designed to equip the saints to hear and act on the word of the Lord for our lives, families, communities, and enterprises.

Life would be directionless, confusing, and frustrating without the guiding voice of God. God spoke to the king's cupbearers at the prison of Egypt, preparing him for his future and He also spoke to Pharaoh in the dream about the future famine and how to avert its harshness (Genesis 40-41). God spoke to Joseph, the Carpenter, about the child his betrothed wife and virgin, Mary, was carrying and helped him not to make the costly mistake of putting away the blessed woman. God revealed the plot of King Herod to kill the child and instructed Joseph to hurry out of Israel to Egypt. When Herod died, God also informed Joseph to travel back to Israel. Every step of the way, he was guided (Mathew 2:13-23). It was not a conversation for just an occasion but a continuous one throughout life. It started a relationship with Joseph on the grassland of Israel among his shepherd brothers; the fellowship was unbroken in the dry pit. This communion kept Joseph focused at the house of Potipher, where his seductive wife constantly tempts him. God spoke to him even in the limiting walls of the prison and gave him prominence and power in the palace and government of the superpower of the ancient world.

CHAPTER SIX
UNDERSTANDING CHANNELS AND METHODS FOR HEARING GOD'S VOICE

Achannel is a mechanism of communication. It is a frequency that we can tune into to hear the voice of God. God employs several means or channels in communicating with us. Although we have identified at least 31 channels in this book, it is important to point out that the unlimited God is in no way constrained to these means. God wants to connect and communicate with us based on our individual design, culture, language, and the paradigms in which we view the world. He knows your inward parts and understands how best to reach you. There are so many voices in the world, so it could sometimes be difficult to differentiate between the voice of God and the other voices that come to us each day. These identified channels will help you understand how to hear God and the ways through which He has been trying to speak to you.

Although we may use one channel and method of God's communication technology individually to receive a message from God, other channels and methods may manifest in synergy simultaneously. In other words, God might use more than one channel to communicate the same thing. The inner witness of the Holy Spirit will be in conformity with the word of God and can sometimes be confirmed by people. In that case, God has employed three different channels to communicate His message: 1. inner witness of the Holy Spirit, 2. the word of God, and 3. people.

Moreover, the secret to enhancing and amplifying our capacity to tune into God and magnify His voice is to employ the Law of Use. What you use frequently, you get more of and what you neglect, you get less of. Consistently communing with God through a specific channel, opens and develops an express passage into the very heart of God. Apostle Paul wrote in Hebrew 5:14 (NKJV), "Solid food belongs to those who are of full age, that is, those who by reason of use have their senses exercised to discern both good and evil." Jesus also states it clearly in Luke 16:10 (NIV), "Whosoever can be trusted with very little can also be trusted with much and whoever is dishonest with very little will also be dishonest with much." In other words, aligning with the channel of communication for connecting to God might not be so express or quick at the beginning. It becomes more potent, stronger, and cordial with time and usage.

There are people who no longer struggle to hear God but that was not always the case. The Prophet Samuel is a good example. The first time God spoke to Samuel, he was a young boy lying in his usual place in the temple. Three times, God called him, and three times, he thought it was Eli, his master (1 Samuel 3-6). Nevertheless, as he grew in the wisdom of God and consistently allowed God to speak to him through the chosen channel, he became conversant with the voice of God and no longer struggled to hear Him. As you identify the channel(s) through which God speaks, it is also necessary to employ the Law of Use to grow and mature in hearing Him, so you no longer have to strain your ears to hear your Father.

METHODS OF OPERATING

There are three common methods of operating God uses to in communicating to us through various channels. They are words, mental imagery, and sensational operations or feelings. Mark Virkler recounts his personal experience of when God or the Holy Spirit was speaking to him. Virkler says that The Holy Spirit functions and manifests through spontaneous thoughts, feelings, visions, or impressions which have a distinct tangibility of God.

Words can comprise audible divine messages. When hearing God's voice audibly, it is crucial to realize that He usually speaks softly. As written in 1Kings 19:12, the Lord passed by gently speaking to Prophet Elijah "in a still small voice." It is important to begin recognizing this method of operation. God is not a loud or forceful Spirit. The Holy Spirit is not just an influence but a reality in the life of a believer. Many of us sometimes mistake the voice of the Spirit with our minds. There are people who think it was them or the devil talking because they have difficulties in recognizing the voice of the Spirit. He speaks to our hearts in a still small voice. Like a gentle whisper, He communicates the heart of God to us.

Your spirit will know the difference between the thoughts or ideas of God from those which are of the devil or developed by the human spirit. Isaiah 52:6 NKJV puts it this way, "Therefore, My people will know My name. Therefore, they shall know in that day that I am He who speaks. 'Behold, it is I.'" So, here the great "I Am" God speaks to us. God assures us in Isaiah 30:21, "Your ears shall hear a word behind you, saying 'This is the way to go, walk in it.'"

Another method God uses to express His messages to us is mental imagery. This is revealed as a vision or something we see. The Bible provides many examples of prophets, apostles, and others who experienced visions from God. In the book of Ezekiel, the Prophet Ezekiel sees and vividly describes visions he saw while in Babylonian captivity with the tribe of Judah. In fact, the whole first chapter is a detailed and colorful description of heavenly beings moving on wheels. One example of Apostle John's vision is in Revelation 4:2-4 NKJV, where he describes viewing God on His throne. "Immediately I was in the Spirit; and behold, a throne set in heaven, and One sat on the throne. And He who sat there was like a jasper and a sardius stone in appearance; and there was a rainbow around the throne, in appearance like an emerald." A vision from God is powerful and can take you anywhere on earth, in heaven, and even in hell. There are Biblical and modern-day testimonies from those who experienced seeing and being present in a God-given vision.

The third method God uses to express His message to us is Sensational Operations which are heartfelt impressions. Divine messages are expressed through physical and emotional stimuli. The recipient of the message can feel when something is right or wrong. It is like a gut feeling that enables one to discern a situation, the motives of a person, or the word and presence of God. Prophet Jeremiah described his sensation saying, "But [His word] was in my heart like a burning fire shut up in my bones; I was weary of holding [it] back, and I could not" (Jeremiah 20:9). Also, Prophet Daniel became physically weak after seeing a troubling vision of the end times. In Daniel 10:10, after encountering Gabriel the messenger angel, he said, "Suddenly, a hand touched me which made me tremble on my knees and on the palms of my hands."

The Holy Spirit can enable us to discern when people are lying. Peter, who was filled with the Holy Spirit, discerned that Ananias and his wife, Sapphira, after selling a possession, kept back part of the proceeds. Although they had not revealed their scheme, Peter, said to Ananias "why has Satan filled your heart to lie to the Holy Spirit and keep back part of the price for yourself?" This was a serious offence in the kingdom of God because at that time believers "had all things in common," meaning no one could "say that any of the things he possessed was his own" (Acts 4:32 NKJV).

CHAPTER SEVEN
CHANNEL 1
SCRIPTURE

So shall My word be that goes forth from My mouth; It shall not return to Me void, But it shall accomplish what I please, And it shall prosper in the thing for which I sent it.
Isaiah 55:11 (NKJV)

Scripture is the infallible word of God given through inspired writers to communicate the mysteries of the kingdom. Scripture also reveals the divine heart of our Creator. Plus, it directs and encourages the Church. Second Timothy 3:16-17 says, "All scripture is given by inspiration of God, and is profitable for doctrine, for reproof, for correction, for instruction in righteousness. That the man of God may be perfect and thoroughly furnished unto all good works."

The 66 books of the Bible reveal God's nature or character and His intelligence provided to humanity, which includes models, principles, and wisdom that are universally applied. The content of this divine book is an expression and revelation of God and His wisdom to the world. It is the greatest book ever written, relevant in all generations and can be personalized irrespective of time, region, or language. The scripture channel gives us direct guidance on many issues. Psalm 12:6 says, "The words of the LORD are flawless, like silver purified in a crucible, like gold refined seven times."

The Scripture is presented to us in the form of Logos, Rhema, and the Hebrew word Dabar. Logos being the spoken word of God as revealed through what has been written. Logos serves as a measuring stick and standard to test all prophetic phenomenon and truth. Jesus said in Matthew 7: 24, "Whoever hears these sayings and does them, I will liken him to a wise man who built his house on the rock." Logos is the general written statements of God on the issues of life. On the other hand, Rhema is the truth spoken and communicated personally to us. Think of Logos as a flowing river and of Rhema as the water fetched from the river in a bucket for your use. Rhema comes by personal revelation or a divine enlightenment for individual benefit. Jesus refer to His word as Rhema when He said, "It is the Spirit who gives life; the flesh profits nothing. The words that I speak to you are spirit, and they are life" (John 6:63). Dabar is a pronounced action word pertaining to God's business at hand. It is the equivalent of the Greek words, Logos and Rhema. Psalm 119:105 (NKJV) says, "Your word is a lamp to my feet and a light to my path."

There are times we are quite confused about certain topics, when we simply need some divine guidance on issues before drawing conclusions or making a decision. The first place to go is the scriptures. We have to search the scriptures for direction, clarity, and understanding. This gives God room to begin to direct and guide us in accordance with His will. We should be like the Bereans who, according to Acts 17: 11, "were more noble minded than the Thessalonians, for they received the message with great eagerness and examined the scriptures every day to see if these teachings were true."

The scripture is the primary channel through which God speaks to us in this dispensation. It is a simple and easy way to access the mind of God and know His verdict on any matter. It is the healthy meal of the soul fit for consumption regardless of one's level of faith and maturity. From a one-day convert, to the leaders of great movements, all of us need to continually turn to the word of God. It is filled with words directly from the mouth of our God. According to 2 Timothy 3:15, all Scripture is given by inspiration of God. It is not the letters and writings of men. If the books of the Bible were words of men, they would be long obsolete and irrelevant in our jet age. But the infallible word of God has transcended all generations becoming newer each day.

The Scriptures were written by men who heard God's voice and were empowered with the privilege of documenting His glorious mysteries for everyone to read and know more about God and the blessings He ordained for us in eternity. Our God is the God of truth and cannot lie, so if He declares that these written words are His, then they are.

However, you must have faith to understand these written mysteries. Beloved, the next time you sit with the word of God to read, know that you are not in any reading competition with anyone. You do not need to be a speed reader when it comes to the word. You should rather be a good listener, patient over the letters as they minister life to you. That is the way to grow and become more established in the faith. It is not about reading the Bible through a year, although that is a noble discipline. It is more important to digest the word of God, meditating on His divine mind and applying it to your life daily. That makes the whole difference. The race in spiritual matters is not really about the strong or swift because the reward is given to the one who endures to the end. You need more endurance to read the Bible than speed.

Call to Me. And I will answer and show you great and unsearchable things
you do not know.
Jeremiah 33: 3

God is ever willing to speak to us. Even as we pray, He will speak and most of the things He says are already contained within the pages of the Scripture. He will never contradict His Word. No matter the channel He uses to reach us, the Bible is still the primary channel. If we claim to have received a message from God and it contradicts or negates the written Word of God, double check because He is not a God of confusion nor is He a God that changes. He is the same yesterday, today and forever. He does not outgrow His words or update His principles for they are perfect in time and eternity.

> *Then I said, "Lord, you know I am suffering for your sake. Punish my persecutors! Don't let them kill me! Be merciful to me and give them what they deserve! Your words are what sustain me. They bring me great joy and are my heart's delight, for I bear your name,*
> *O Lord God Almighty.*
> Jeremiah 15:15-16 NLT

Jeremiah was in a very uncomfortable situation and the young prophet was so lost in despair that he prayed for the misfortune of his enemies. But when he discovered the words of God, he hungrily devoured them. His heart was overwhelmed with joy and unspeakable peace. That is what the word does. It heals the wounds of the heart, puts our visions in perspective, and sets us in alignment with God's divine purpose. It was the word (the sword of the Spirit) that Jesus used in confronting the tempter. Matthew 4:3-4 (KJV) says, "And when the tempter came to him, he said, 'If thou be the Son of God, command that these stones be made bread.' But he answered and said, 'It is written, Man shall not live by bread alone, but by every word that proceedeth out of the mouth of God.'" Be a student of the word and your breakthrough in the things of the Spirit will come easy with less struggles.

CHANNEL 2
PRAYER AND FASTING

Moses was there with the LORD forty days and forty nights without eating bread or drinking water. And he wrote on the tablets the words of the covenant,
the Ten Commandments.
Exodus 34: 28 NIV

Praying and fasting is a healthy combination of spiritual activity to condition the spirit and soul in readiness to receive from God. Prayer compliments fasting because it is the prime channel for initiating communication with God. So, while praying, we can petition God to bless the fast and cause it to be pleasing to Him, as well as other requests. As we pray, our ears are opened, our hearts are more receptive to absorb the inspiration of God, and our spirits are more aligned to go higher in Him. Prayer breaks up the fallow ground of the heart, so that with the watering of Scripture, the planted seed of fasting produces a harvest of benefits. God rewards our earnest sacrifice of fasting as Isaiah 58:8 says, "Then your light shall break forth like the morning, your healing shall spring forth speedily…"

The Holy Spirit can stir you up to do away with food and pleasure for a while. He can encourage you to sit with the Scripture in an atmosphere where there are no distractions, in order to receive expressly from God. Fasting weakens the body and consequently reduces its activities while prayer gives us a spiritual focus, setting the spotlight on God. Because our body is weak for lack of food and water, we are less likely to be busy with distractions.

The discipline of fasting can heighten spiritual sensitivity through the reduction of natural activities like eating and drinking. It is a means for spiritual elevation and clarity, enabling access to lofty realms in the Spirit. Moses was with God for forty days and nights without food and mysteries of the kingdom were revealed, plus the laws of God were made plain to him. Jesus also fasted for forty days and nights (Luke 4:2-4). Apostles, prophets, kings, priests, other leaders all fasted at one point or another to access the heart of God (Ezra 8:21-23, Jonah 3:5-9,2 Samuel 1:12, Acts 13:2, Daniel 10:3, Esther 4:16).

As a modern servant-leader of God, I (Dr. Haupt) learnt that applying this discipline in my personal life has the unprecedented power to transform me more and more into all that God has ordained for me. Also, I discovered that the principle of fasting is a powerful channel through which God uses to open up His office for business and vision meetings which He uses communicate with us.

CHANNEL 3
WORSHIP ACTS

Worship is another channel to discern the mind of God and His purpose for your life. Worship is a way of attributing reverence, honor, or just paying respect and homage to God. Worship has been a big part of my (Prophet Dorothy) life. Because most of us love music, so it is one of the main ways we tune in to and worship God. But as I grew in my relationship with God, I discovered that prayer is a way of worshiping God. Just sitting and listening is a way of worshiping God. Jesus made it clear in John 4:23, that "the hour is coming, and now is, when the true worshipers will worship the Father in spirit and in truth; for of worshipers the Father is seeking such to worship Him. God is Spirit, and His worshipers must worship Him in spirit and in truth."

Always make worship a part of your life every day. Worship should be a daily activity. Just like the scripture says in 1 Thessalonians 5:17, "pray without ceasing," you should also worship without ceasing. This is because worship is what keeps God on the throne of your heart. Praise raises Him up there, but worship keeps Him on the throne. Praise is about thanking God for what He has already done while worship is adoring Him for who He is. It is an exploration and a celebration of His very nature. When the Kings wanted to hear from the Lord, they would often say, "Go get me a minstrel." The minstrel (musician and/or singer) can use worship to change the atmosphere from natural to supernatural.

When I (Dr. Haupt) want to meet with God, I do not always have to wait until God comes to me. I can go visit God by worshiping and praising Him. And one of the habits that I have learned to do in my life is to be intentional about connecting with God. Learning and calling God's redemptive names is quite helpful in communing with Him. Only His friends really use those names.

We can become friends of God by getting to know Him on an intimate level. Knowing and calling Him by His uniquely redemptive names can cause this most important relationship to become so personal. Like the Israelites would sometimes call Him Jehovah Jireh (the Lord, my Provider), Genesis 22:14; Jehovah Rapha (the Lord, my Healer), Exodus 15:26; Jehovah Nissi (the Lord, my Banner), Exodus 17:15; Jehovah Shalom, (the Lord, my Peace), Judges 6:24; Jehovah Rohi (the Lord my Shepherd), Psalms 23; Jehovah Tsidkenu (the Lord my Righteousness), Jeremiah 23:6 and Jeremiah 33:16; and Jehovah Shammah, (the Lord that is there), Ezekiel 48:35.

When you become a worshiper, who is close with God, like a bride and groom, you enter into levels of intimacy with Him. Then, you will begin to discern the power of worship, using it as an open channel. My (Dr. Haupt) relationship with God, especially in worship, is not a monologue but dialogue where we exchange conversations. Understand, worship is more like the foreplay between lovers. This is what happens when you get to the real deal. You do not obtain direction from God or hear God's voice unless you engage in the foreplay of praise and worship.

CHAPTER EIGHT
CHANNEL 4
MEDITATIONS

Blessed is the one who does not walk in step with the wicked or stand in the way that sinners take or sit in the company of mockers, but whose delight is in the law of the LORD, and who meditates on his law day and night. That person is like a tree planted by streams of water, which yields its fruit in season and whose leaf does not wither—whatever they do prospers. Not so the wicked! They are like chaff that the wind blows away. Therefore, the wicked will not stand in the judgment, nor sinners in the assembly of the righteous. For the LORD watches over the way of the righteous, but the way of the wicked leads to destruction.
Psalm 1:1–6 NIV

Meditation is the practice of mindfulness, concentration, and focusing on a particular object, thought or activity. Meditation is a healthy spiritual practice recommended by God Himself in Joshua 1: 8 when He says, "This book of the law shall not depart from your mouth, but you shall meditate on it day and night, so that you may be careful to do according to all that is written in it; for then you will make your way prosperous, and then you will have success."

Open the Bible and read the verse or verses you plan to meditate on. Spend as much time as you need to gain a basic understanding of the words, then bookmark the verse for later. You will need to refer to it continually throughout your meditation. After reading through the passage, read it again. Meditation opens up mysteries and allows the Holy Spirit to minister wisdom, healing, ideas, and revelations to you. As you meditate on the word of God, you are fellowshipping with the Holy Spirit. What a sweet experience we have while meditating!

One of the neglected powers in the body of Christ is the ability to meditate. We often associate the channel of meditation with the New Age, but it is actually a biblical practice that God uses to visit us and release His thoughts, His purposes and His intentions. Meditation is an incredible practice that was practiced by all our spiritual forefathers.

The Hebrew word for meditate is haga (pronounced haw-gaw), which means to muttered or murmur; to speak in a low an audible voice with oneself. A lot of us meditate and don't even realize it because it occurs as we self-talk. Have you ever sat in a room talking something over and over with yourself, or thinking something over and over? That was an act of meditation. The scripture tells us to meditate on the word of God. There is a power generated when we do that. We often meditate on our fears and what we do not want. But when we meditate on what God wants for us through the revelation of His scriptures, the Holy Spirit speaks to us. This can produce some incredible results in our lives.

The scripture tells us in 3 John 1:2, "Beloved, I pray that you may prosper in all things and be in health, just as your soul prospers." Your soul is made up of your emotions, will, and intellect. And when we begin to use the practice of meditation in our devotional life, it will enhance our hearing, seeing, and senses of what the will of God is.

Please understand, this is part of God's science. So, meditate to tap into communications from God's realm. It is time for the saints to utilize the channel of meditation, particularly with the scriptures and reap its benefits. Consider that the world offers classes, training, courses, and accommodations for practicing meditation while the Church does not. We should have meditation rooms in churches where people come and learn not only how to pray, but how to meditate. Meditation will take our prayer life from being a monologue to an actual dialogue. The channel of meditation is valuable to us in discerning the mind of God.

Isaiah 26:3 says, "You will keep in perfect peace those whose minds are steadfast because they trust in you." Philippians 4:8 also says, "Finally brothers and sisters, whatever is true, whatever is noble, whatever is right, whatever is pure, whatever is lovely, but it's admirable. If anything is excellent or praiseworthy, think about such things, meditate on such things, and He will keep you in perfect peace." Meditation is something that you must practice and be intentional about.

Meditation is a lost prophetic art of the saints. This is a tool that I (Dr. Haupt) use to initiate communications with God. There are times in prayer when I just say "God, I want to hear what you want to say about my marriage, my children, my finances, my job." I began a meditation on what God has said in his written word and what He has said to me through prophecies.

We need to think of prayer differently; something we do as an obligation. Actually, I love the late Dr. Myles Munroe's definition of prayer. He said, "Prayer is giving God license to interfere with our affairs." Prayer is not just us asking for things, but it is legislating, communicating, meditating, and conducting business with God. It is engaging in a conversation with God that really causes Him to talk to us. God is a responsive personality. When you begin to talk to Him, it is His nature to respond. Matthew 7:11 declares, " If you then, being evil, know how to give good gifts to your children, how much more will your Father who is in Father give the Holy Spirit to those who ask Him! So, an essential channel for opening up communication with God starts with prayer.

CHANNEL 5
SILENCE

So then, my beloved brethren, let everyone man be swift to hear, slow to
speak, slow to wrath.
James 1:19 NKJV

Silence is the channel that engages the act of fasting words and sounds. The practice of sacrificing those human impulses and expressions are instrumental in connecting us to God's wavelength of wordless communications. Jesus occasionally withdrew to a quiet place where He could connect with God without any interruption. He sometimes would rise before dawn or send everyone away, so He could be alone. The Bible says in Mark 1:35, "Now in the morning, having risen a long while before daylight, He went out and departed into a solitary place, and there He prayed." This channel is similar to meditation but while it is possible to meditate almost anywhere, withdrawing from noise and distraction to a completely quiet environment was one of the ways through which Jesus connected with God the Father during His ministry on earth. We should explore this wonderful aspect to commune with God in solitude.

CHANNEL 6
JOURNALING

Journaling is the devotional practice of keeping a personal record of meditations, reflections, occurrences, and experiences on a regular basis. One of the most valuable tools operational in our lives is the devotional habit of journaling. Writing what one hears during time with God in prayer and in meditation and documenting other significant experiences is journaling. This is a personal life account recorded through the logos or written words. Proverbs 7:3 says to treasure God's commandments within you, and "write them on the tablet of your heart." Journaling is a personalized way to create spiritual records for immediate and future reference, documenting the voice and intention of God that may otherwise be forgotten.

This is a common practice among most victorious Christians. They keep track of what God impresses on their hearts, which serves as a constant guide and reminder of God's personal messages and lessons to them. Like a Chinese adage says, "The faintest ink is better than the sharpest memory." Through the act of journaling, we can capture the mind of God in a written form. If you think about it, the Bible is one big journal written by a lot of people. They simply took what God said to them and wrote it down.

God instructed the Prophet Habakkuk to write down the vision. Habakkuk 2:2 (NIT) says, "Then the LORD answered me: 'Write down this vision and clearly inscribe it on tablets, so that a herald may run with it. For the vision awaits an appointed time; it testifies of the end and does not lie. Though it lingers, wait for it, since it will surely come and not delay." You are not going to get the resources needed to complete your purpose by just storing everything that God told you in your mind, trusting your memory.

I (Dorothy) started journaling early in my Christian walk. I realized I was not going to remember everything God was telling me if I had to commit His sacred messages to memory alone. I began to document the mind of God as He spoke to me and there were times after a year or two, when He said similar things. I would quickly go back to my journal and check what God had said in the past for guidance and more clarity.

Journaling is very important because our brains are not wired to hold everything we see, hear, or feel and accurately comprehend it right then. However, by writing it down, we can be fairly accurate about what happened.

Habakkuk was a prophet, seeking to hear God about the contradiction of what he was seeing with his eyes. His natural world experience was not lining up with God's intention, so Habakkuk went to a quiet place and began to hear God's thoughts and record them. Journaling is a written record of how and what God has been working and saying in our lives. God may speak to us about something today that might not manifest for another ten years. But God wants us to get into the intimate act of valuing and documenting His thoughts and words on paper. A lot of us struggle with writing. I (Dr. Haupt) am one of the people who finds writing difficult because I often find it easier to verbalize my thoughts than to write them. Although I am a right-brain oriented person, I understand the value and power of journaling from people like Prophet Dorothy, who has blessed me to take deliberate steps in documenting my personal dealings with God.

God wants you to write down what He says or impresses on your heart for the future. As you fellowship with God, keep your diary or journal close and be ready to write down the things He says. This practice will bless you beyond words.

CHAPTER NINE
CHANNEL 7
PRECEPT UPON PRECEPT

*Whom shall He teach knowledge? And whom shall He make to understand
doctrine? Them that are weaned from the milk, and drawn from the breasts.
For precept must be upon precept; line upon line, line upon line;
here a little, and there a little.*
Isaiah 28: 9-10 KJV

Precept is defined as a command or principle intended, especially as a general rule of action. It is an order issued by a legally constituted authority to a subordinate official. God does not reveal all His mysteries in one conversation. He takes time moving from the simplest to the most complex. Isaiah 28:9-10 makes it clear that God teaches knowledge and makes spiritual doctrine explicit to those who have been weaned from the milk and those who are drawn from the breast. In other words, there are levels of spiritual maturity that qualifies you for certain revelations and encounters.

In the kingdom, growth is paramount, and you must take it seriously to enjoy more of God. For precept must be upon precept and line upon line. Your growth and experience of God must be gradual and continuous. God might be dealing with anger, bitterness, and forgiveness in the heart of a young Christian, while He is teaching a more matured one to love and pray for the good of his enemies. Therefore, we must be attentive to what God is saying in a particular season, knowing that everything He is trying to teach us is connected to a deeper and bigger purpose and principle. This makes an essential case for the restoration of Sunday school and mid-week Bible study, which enhances our understanding.

CHANNEL 8
FRUIT OF THE SPIRIT

"But the fruit of the Spirit is love, joy, peace, patience, kindness, goodness, faithfulness, gentleness and self-control. Against such things there is no law."
Galatians 5: 22-23 NIV

The power and the presence of the Holy Spirit produces the spiritual fruit written in the scripture above. The observing world sees and is blessed by those who bear spiritual fruit but usually do not give attributions to God. Many lives have been touched and many souls won for Christ through simple acts of love, joy, peace, kindness, faithfulness, and all the other fruit of the Spirit. There are times when lengthy sermons are not needed. All one needs to do is express the fruit of the Spirit and people will be blessed. They will be able to hear the loving voice of the Maker and see the bleeding Christ on the cross through our compassionate expressions. Their hearts may be kindled to want to know more, or they might be convicted of sin and try to seek forgiveness as we show the

CHANNEL 9
AUDIBLE VOICE

God sometimes speaks through the audible voice. Although it is not among the most common channels through which God speaks to us, it is still one of the means confirmed many times in the Bible. He spoke to the prophets directly on many occasions in the Old Testament. He spoke to Apostle Paul through the audible voice on the way to Damascus. "And I fell unto the ground, and heard a voice saying to me, Saul, Saul, why persecutest thou me?" (Acts 22:7 KJV). We also read in Luke 3:22, "The Holy Spirit descended upon Him [Jesus] in bodily form, as a dove, and a voice came from heaven, which said, 'Thou are my beloved Son; in thee I am well pleased." There are people who converse with God directly, but this is not usually the case for most people. It has been said earlier that God speaks to us in accordance to the way we are wired and designed. If you have to wait solely on hearing the audible voice of God, you might have to wait for a very long time.

CHAPTER TEN
CHANNEL 10
FAITH

*Trust in the Lord with all your heart, and lean not to your own
understanding. In all your ways acknowledge Him, and He will direct your
paths.*
Proverbs 3: 5-6 NKJV

We can connect with the heart through the acts of faith. It is written in John 7:38 that whoever believes in God, rivers of living water will flow within them. Faith and confidence in God create a channel of communication and allows us to access His will expressly. Faith connects us to God and keeps us in shape for the fulfillment of our purposes in Christ. In fact, it is impossible to please God without faith. Anyone who must come or connect with God must believe He exists and that He rewards those who earnestly seek Him (Hebrews 11: 6). No matter how discouraging the days might be and even when blanketed by sheets of somber clouds, we must never doubt the faithfulness of God. Faithlessness disconnects us from the heart of the Father.

Faith is essential to adequately function in the kingdom of God on earth. Faith is required to carry out our assignments from God and it comes to life through the work we do. As James 2:26 confirms, "For as the body without the spirit is dead, so faith without works is dead also." So, faith is a mandatory channel for hearing the Voice of God and as Romans 12:3 says, "God has dealt to each one a measure of faith." The Law of Use can be applied to faith, too, because like a muscle, the more you use it, the stronger it becomes.

CHANNEL 11
WORD KNOWLEDGE

For to one is given the word of wisdom through the Spirit, and to another the word
of knowledge through the same Spirit.
1 Corinthians 12: 8 NKJV

The word of knowledge is when the Holy Spirit makes known to you things that ordinarily you have no knowledge or awareness of. It is the supernatural insight given to us by the Holy Spirit. God speaks to us through the word of knowledge, which is one of the nine gifts of the Spirit (1Corithians 12:1-10). In Acts 5:1-11, Ananias and Sapphira had gone out and sold a piece of land only to come before the apostles and lie about the profit. The Holy Spirit revealed to Peter their secret sins and they could not deny it. Many Christians operate in the word of knowledge and they do not even know it. When you receive an insight on how to go about a thing or your heart is inspired to discover an answer, God is speaking *to* you and *through* you concerning the situations around you. It could be an idea on how to start a business, a direction in choosing your future spouse, how to resolve a social, organizational, or marital dispute, or perhaps, where you have misplaced your car keys.

Word of knowledge is another unique channel through which God speaks to us. Word of knowledge is a *word* of information not always a *chapter* of information. This channel by its very nature often require synergy with other channels because its information is often partial and not complete. So, it could be a piece of information made known that could bring clarity, confirmation, or connect the dots concerning a situation.

CHANNEL 12
WORD OF WISDOM

Get wisdom, get understanding...
Proverbs 4:5-7 NIV

While the word of knowledge comes as a revelation of what is unknown; the word of wisdom helps us to appropriately apply knowledge in various situations. This spiritual gift is the wisdom of God imparted into many saints to prepare God's people as vision partners who discover purpose, identify priorities, to attain the heights He calls us to achieve. The word of wisdom is strategically important in implementing the business and dreams that God gives you. Apostle Paul wrote in 1 Corinthians 2:6-7 (NKJV), "However, we speak wisdom among those who are mature, yet not the wisdom of this age, nor of the rulers of this age, who are coming to nothing. But we speak the wisdom of God in a mystery, the hidden wisdom which God ordained before the ages for our glory." The life of a child of God is defined by godly wisdom. It is one of the blessings of redemption to walk and operate in dimensions of excellence that awes the world. According to Exodus 31:3, you are filled with the Spirit of God, in wisdom, understanding, knowledge and skills in all you do.

God is not limited to the temple or church buildings. He is interested in motivating and positioning you to function and flow in all the ecosystems of his kingdom here on earth. The wisdom of God is a word or an inspiration from God that guides you into all that is meant for you.

CHANNEL 13

THE GIFT OF DISCERNING SPIRITS

The gift of discernment is the gift of insight, clear judgement, and understanding. It is one of the most essential gifts a child of God could have to triumph in the world. Discernment cuts through deception like a sword and those who possess it can avoid a lot trouble. Discerning in Greek is diakrisis, which means judging through the idea or seeing through a plain and outward concept. It can guide you into the heart and will of God and help you to see through a situation. For instance, in the case of Prophet Samuel when he visited the house of Jesse to anoint one of his sons as the second king of Israel. "The LORD said to Samuel, 'Do not consider his appearance or his height, for I have rejected him. The LORD does not look at things people at. People look at the outward appearance, but the LORD looks at the heart'" (1 Samuel 16:7). The Spirit of discernment fills us with the divine wisdom to understand the deep and hidden things of God. The Bible says in Proverbs 18:15, "The heart of the discerning acquires knowledge, for the ears of the wise seek it out."

The gift of discernment, one of the channels God uses, is a supernatural energy motivated by the Holy Spirit to see beyond the natural or physical. It removes the veil from our eyes and makes secret things plain. When this Spirit is operative in a believer, he or she is able to see through the natural into the realm of the Spirit to recognize the source of spirits and ascertain whether they are of God, satanic, or human.

We are encouraged by Apostle John not to believe every spirit, "but test the spirits to see whether they are from God" (1 John 4:1). The Tyndale Dictionary defines discernment as "the wisdom to recognize truths from untruths by correctly evaluating whether a behavior or teaching is from God, the devil, or human motivation."

Remember, these highlighted channels for accessing the spontaneous flow of God's direction and wisdom often work in tandem with each other. For instance, when you have the gift of discernment, God will often give you a word of knowledge about facts and information you need to know in order to discern. God may provide a word of wisdom on how to handle a particular manifestation of discernment.

The discernment is a gift that should be at work in all of us most of the time, but at least some of the time. Do not forget, this gift is empowered by the Holy Spirit. Without the Holy Spirit, the lives of believers would be barren and bankrupt of fruit and gifts of the Spirit. The Bible says, "He (the Holy Spirit) gives some the ability to discern whether a message is from the Spirit of God or from another spirit" (1 Corinthians 12:10). He gives some the power to perform miracles, others the ability to prophesy, and bestows other gifts appropriately as well.

Discernment for you is crucial in making decisions. The Old Testament model of this gift in operation was generally used by the prophets and the priests. And it was through an instrument called the Urim and Thummim. God instructed Moses to "Put the Urim and Thummim in the breastplate, so they will be over Aaron's heart whenever he enters the presence of the Lord. So, Aaron will always bear the means of making decisions for the Israelites over his heart before the Lord" (Exodus 28:30).

Discerning of Spirits is the Sensory Perception Function of a believer that helps in detecting what God wants you to know. It is often connected to God helping the receiver identify the type of the spirit behind a circumstance. We must be able to discern what spirits are operating because it is possible to have a spirit telling you something good, but with a selfish motive. We all need the gift of discernment because it is a safeguard against deception. Peter discerned that Simon the magician's motives were wrong when he asked for the Holy Spirit. He was trying to hijack the gifts of the Spirit for ill-gotten gain. Paul was also able to discern that the spirit in Elymas the sorcerer was not of God but of the devil (Acts 13:9-12).

The gift of discernment will help us to pick the right people, places, and teams to be on. I (Dr. Haupt) had a Christian friend and we worked in ministry together. But when we were around each other, I discerned our chemistry together would either promote us to be righteous or sinful. This helped me to use wisdom in my interaction with that friend. Discernment can come to us as a flash of revelation in our thoughts or a gut feeling. It can be a vision or a slight mental impression. It can be a prophetic flow of words, audible or inaudible. The goal of the information is to help us see beyond the natural veil. It is a gift we need to flow in because we inhabit this world and there are so many different confusing and misleading spirits here. The ability to discern is a divine defense mechanism to filter the spirits and distinguish which one is from God. It protects the saints from deception and equips us to make right choices.

CHAPTER ELEVEN
CHANNEL 14
AGENCY OF THE HOLY SPIRIT

God is Spirit, and those who worship Him must worship in spirit and in truth.
John 4:24 NKJV

One of the most dynamic intelligence agents that God the Father has on the planet is The Holy Spirit of God. He is the most treasured partner, the most reliable friend, and the most trusted ally of the redeemed. The Holy Spirit is God dwelling within and with us. He is the channel or agency of God in motion known in Hebrew as Ruach and in Greek as Pneuma. This channel or the Agency of the Holy Spirit is a phenomenon of God's divine power working *in*, *upon*, and *around* us to communicate His intelligence.

The Holy Spirit and the written words are both the primary channels through which God talks to us. John 4:24 reveals that those who worship God must do so in Spirit and in truth. In other words, the spirit of the redeemed communes with the Spirit of God. The Holy Spirit is the abiding presence of God on earth and as children of God, our spirits are connected to Him in such a way that communication flows seamlessly between us. The Holy

Spirit mediates between us and our heavenly Father, and there may be times of some confusion on certain things. No problem. The Holy Spirit is able to translate our feelings adequately and relate with our emotions effectively. We read in Romans 8:26 that there are times we might groan with feelings that cannot be uttered but the Spirit expressly communicates our hearts to God. While God is in heaven and we are on earth, the Holy Spirit occupies both and therefore forms an authoritative channel of communication between God and His children.

The manifestation of the Spirit is given to each one for the profit of all: for to one is given the word of wisdom through the Spirit, to another the word of knowledge through the Spirit, to another faith by the same Spirit, to another gifts of healings by the same Spirit, to another the working of miracles, to another prophecy, to another discerning of the Spirits, to another different kinds of tongues, to another the interpretation of tongues. But to one and the same Spirit works all these things, distributing to each one individually as He wills.
1 Corinthians 12: 7-11 NKJV

The Holy Spirit works in and through us. He helps us to grow into the maturity of our spiritual gifts. We are guided in the path of destiny by the agency of the Holy Spirit. He can be rightfully called the most important Person on earth because His presence enables us to live holy and function with power in a troubled and fallen world. He is the Voice of God speaking *to* and *through* us while keeping, guiding, and even convicting us when we are wrong. Learn to hear The Holy Spirit, the voice of God, because He is God present with us.

CHANNEL 15
AGENCY OF THE PROPHET AND SEER

For when David was up in the morning, the word of the LORD came unto the prophet Gad, David's seer, saying, "Go and say unto David, thus saith the LORD, I offer you three things; choose thee one of them, that I may do it unto thee."
2 Samuel 24: 11-12

God sometimes speaks to His beloved through the prophets. This was common among judges and kings of the Old Testament. Remember Elijah and Ahab, Samuel and Saul, Nathan and David? Prophets are endowed with the supernatural ability to see things that are unknown and predict things that will certainly come to pass. God has raised men and women in that capacity in the body of Christ for the purpose of communication with the Church . Yet, it is important to stress that this is not the primary means of God's communication with us.

The messages delivered to us by the prophets should be tried and measured with the word of God. In 1 Kings 13:11-25, a serious lesson on obedience is provided by interaction between a young and an old prophet. The young prophet had already received direct words from God not to eat or drink or turn back from his way, but he was deceived by the old prophet who came under the pretext that he was sent by God. He obeyed the old prophet without double checking and that led to his death. God might speak to you through a prophet but that will never be his primary means of communicating with you. Why does He go through a prophet when He can speak to you directly?

CHANNEL 16

AGENCY OF THE HUMAN SPIRIT OR PEOPLE

For by wise counsel you will wage your own war, and in a multitude of counselors there is safety.
Proverbs 24: 6 NKJV

God can also choose to speak to you through another person. This might come in the form of wise counsel or advice from a spouse, friend, family member, an elder, business partner, a colleague, and others. It is one of the valid channels employed by God to communicate with His children down through the ages. It should be taken more seriously, especially when it comes from a member of the household of faith and should be scrutinized with the word of God to check if it is in conformity with God's precepts. Members of the body of Christ can and should function in harmony and synergy to the glory of our God (1 Corinthians 12:18, Romans 12:5).

Scriptures say that God sets us into the body in a way that pleases Him. Therefore, we are joints connected to one another. There are people that God deliberately put in your life for your growth, development, maturity, and support. Also, God allows people into your life who may test, try, and enhance your patience, which are usually uncomfortable relationships that make you stronger and more resilient. Some, God may put in your life because of one unique destiny to help you to understand and validate what you have been through; to question or clarify the things that you perceive God may be speaking to you. It is important to begin to understand and acknowledge that these people have a place in your life because you may be chosen by God to minister to them in an area of hurt, pain, or brokenness that God delivered you out of. And there are some sent to minister to you but regardless, God is usually speaking to you in some way through the people in your life. So, pay attention, observe and listen.

In Exodus 18, we see how Jethro counsels Moses to make sound administrative decisions by sharing the leadership responsibilities among qualified individuals. Without that wise counsel, he would have crashed under the weight of leadership. Even though Moses was a prophet who spoke to God face to face, God still spoke through his father-in-law to instruct and guide him in the right direction.

As young Timothy grew in grace, we often read of how Apostle Paul would encourage him (1 Timothy 1:2,18-20, 1 Corinthians 4:17). God appoints pastors after His own heart to watch the sheep (Jeremiah 3:15). Ruth had Naomi (Ruth 1:6-20), Esther had Mordecai (Esther 2:5-7), Pharaoh had Joseph (Genesis 41:14-44), and Nebuchadnezzar had Daniel (2:24-48). There are people God has stationed on your path as you go through life to keep pointing you to the right direction towards your destiny. Our heavenly Father often uses human agents to relate universal and scientific principles that confirm His truths.

Nevertheless, this channel comes with precautions. Please test every spirit to discern which is from God and which is not (1Corinthians 13:12). Avoid giving the human agent God's status. No matter what you go through, be patient to verify what people say to you with the word of God.

For example, marriages can go through the worst of times. When my husband and I (Prophet Dorothy) got married, I was only 18.

We have been married for 47 years and we have survived some marital trials, especially at the beginning of our marriage. We did not start out seeking God because it was more of mutual affection than the actual love built on the foundation of faith. But when the challenges of marriage began to set in, God raised people to continually pray for us. Through the power of the Holy Spirit and the help of God's human agents we were able to overcome and we are still overcoming today. Of course, you should not expect so much from the last kid of the family and a young high school graduate. I was young and naïve, but God sent His words through people that changed the trajectory of our lives for better. The unlimited God can even use our enemies if need be. God might send His words of change through educational systems, social groups, or organizational structures. We know, according to Proverbs 27:17, that iron sharpens iron.

CHANNEL 17
AGENCY OF ANGELS

For He will command His angels concerning you
to guard you in all your ways.
Psalm 91: 11 NIV

Angels are spiritual beings functioning in various capacities and some of them are divine messengers, agents, or emissaries sent to conduct business on the behalf of God in the affairs of men. Angels, according to Hebrews 1:14, are ministering spirits to believers, usually performing specific functions as ordained by God. The Hebrew word for angel is Malack and in Greek, it is called Aggelos.

Angels are holy beings devoted to God. They operate individually or inside of an agency. The agency of angels is a valid biblical channel of divine communication. However, this must be handled with caution as well because God's preferred choices of communication include His Word, the Holy Spirit, and people. Historically and as portrayed vividly in the Scriptures, angels prefer not to be seen because they are created to bring glory to God and serve His purpose without drawing attention to themselves.

Nevertheless, we should not be ignorant of the fact that there are other fallen angels who are not dedicated to God. These are demons of darkness dedicated to do the bidding of Satan. They are the messengers of Lucifer, the fallen Star. Angelic ministry is a very powerful channel for God's messages and intervention in our lives.

CHANNEL 18
AGENCY OF COMMUNITY

Our immediate community can become a channel through which God communicates His intentions and will to us. We are social beings and the community we associate with will influence the direction we face in life. There are people blessed through associations while some are wounded by the company they keep. God can create a culture within your community, drop an idea among the people, and initiate a movement within the group. By being a member of that group, you are indirectly aligning with the purpose of God for your life. This is why it is important to know which community or group you allow to influence you. Not all influences or ideas coming from the community are from God, some are distractions to destiny. Therefore, you must be able to discern the right messages from the unhealthy messages coming from any community you are part of.

CHANNEL 19
AGENCY OF NATURE

There are four things on earth that are small but unusually wise: Ants—they aren't strong, but they store up food for the winter. Rock badgers—they aren't powerful, but they make their homes among the rocky cliffs. Locusts—they have no king, but they march in formation ... Lizards—they are easy to catch, but they are found even in kings' palaces.
Proverbs 30:24-28 NLT

Another of the channel that God often uses to talk to us is through nature. God sometimes uses the inanimate and living things from our natural environment to speak deep mysteries and reveal His great wisdom. For example, in Proverbs 6:6, He says, "Go to the ant, you sluggard; consider its ways and be wise! It has no commander, no overseer or ruler, yet it stores its provisions in summer and gathers its food in harvest." By merely observing the ants, you can know what God has to say to you in kairos time or season. In the case mentioned in Proverbs 6, it was a message and instruction on diligence. Jesus talks about the flowers of the field clothed in beauty and the birds of the sky sufficiently cared for in Matthew 6: 30 to emphasize our need of faith and trust in God. Solomon said, look at the ant. Observing the ant can reveal life principals God wants you to know. Also, the scriptures talk to us about eagles and what they do. The admirable and soaring traits of an eagle is conveyed in Isaiah 40:31. "But those who wait on the Lord shall renew their strength; they shall mount up with wings like eagles, they shall run and not be weary, they shall walk and not faint." God will use creatures and things in nature to speak to us and validate how he brings together insights and principles that we can apply.

Proverbs 6:6-11 NLT says, "Take a lesson from the ants, you lazybones. Learn from their ways and become wise!" By merely looking at this model in the environment, we can access Godly wisdom which will open our hearts, eyes, and ears to perceive messages from God not thought of ordinarily.

CHAPTER THIRTEEN
CHANNEL 20
DREAMS

*When they had gone, an angel of the Lord appeared to Joseph in a dream.
"Get up," he said, "take the child and his mother and escape to Egypt. Stay
there until I tell you, for Herod is going to search for the child to kill him."*
Matthew 2:13 NIV

Science tends to define dreams as a series of thoughts, images, and sensations occurring in a person's mind during sleep. However, God occasionally seizes our time of rest to speak to us as we sleep. Unlike visions, during which you do not have to be asleep, dreams come when you are partially or completely unconscious and unaware of your physical environment. It is very natural to dream just as it is natural to think or talk. The same way God can take hold of your heart to inspire your thoughts or overshadow you to utter prophetic mysteries, He can also speak to you through dreams. Joseph the Carpenter was primarily spoken to and guided through dreams to make the right decisions every step of the way. It was through a dream that he knew the truth about Mary's pregnancy. God revealed the intentions of Herod to him concerning the child Messiah and instructed him on what to do through dreams (Matthew 2: 13). He was also informed about the death of Herod through a dream (Matthew 2: 19).

God gave Joseph, the eleventh son of Jacob, a glimpse, and an understanding of his destiny through dreams. At Bethel, Jacob had a dream that redirected his focus and realigned his wandering feet in the direction of his calling (Genesis 28: 10-22). Daniel was so blessed that he not only dreamed but could dream the dream of another person and interpret it. The book of Daniel, chapter 2 recounts how God revealed the unknown or forgotten dream of King Nebuchadnezzar to Daniel. God gave him the special ability to understand dreams (Daniel 1: 17).

There are several other instances in the Bible where God communicates with humans through dreams. This is not the primary way through which God communicates and all dreams must still be verified in the light of His words to insure they do not negate His laws or contradict His promises. You may want to watch out for such divine encounters through dreams.

CHANNEL 21
VISIONS

*And it shall come to pass in the last days, says God, that I will pour out
of My Spirit on all flesh; your sons and your daughters shall prophesy, your
young men shall see visions, your old men shall dream dreams.*
Acts 2: 17 NKJV

Visions, like prophecy, is one of the channels through which God
speaks to us. They are exclusively unique in experience. Prophecy
can be a divine inspiration or an overwhelming presence of God,
causing His human messenger to make utterances directly from
Him that are not premeditated. On the other hand, visions do not
necessarily require the human vessel to speak. While prophecy
deals primarily with the mouth, vision has to do with the sight.
This is when God opens your eyes to see and hear things or engage
a realm that is not accessible to the natural man. The end result of
vision could be prophetic (talking about the future), clarify doubts,
or encourage a weary soul, such as in the case of Apostle Paul.

We can see from Acts 18: 9-10 how the Lord appeared to
Apostle Paul in a vision saying "Do not be afraid, but speak, do
not be silent; for I am with you, and no one will attack to hurt you;
for I have many people in this city." Unlike the edifying vision of
Apostle Paul, Prophet Daniel's vision was prophetic in Daniel 7:
13-14. Daniel recounts his experience saying, "I looked, and there
before me was one like a son of man, coming with the clouds
of heaven. He approached the Ancient of Days and was led into
His presence. He was given authority, glory and sovereign power;

all nations and peoples of every language worshiped Him. His dominion is an everlasting dominion that will not pass away, and his kingdom is one that will never be destroyed." Here Daniel was able to see the glorified Christ taking His position in eternity after the work of salvation for the world was perfected on the cross.

God spoke to Apostle Peter, the Centurion, and others through vision and He is still opening the eyes of many of His people today. God is enabling them to see and hear things about their lives, generation, and the future. Never forget that this is not the primary way through which God communes with us. The still small voice of the Holy Spirit, the written word of God, and the agency of the brethren (apostle, prophets, pastors, brothers and sisters in the faith) are still God's primary channels for reaching us irrespective of our level of spiritual maturity. It is perfectly normal if God is not speaking to you through visions or through prophecy.

CHANNEL 22
PROPHECY

For prophecy never came by the will of man, but holy men of God spoke as they were moved by the Holy Spirit.
2 Peter 1:21 NKJV

The gift of prophecy is a particularly important gift provided by God to the Church. We must recognize its operation because prophecy is a very pivotal function for moving in action to effectively accomplish what God has called us to do. The ability for each individual to be able to hear God's voice and decree that information to receivers or to use it, is important. One of the best writers on this gift of prophecy is a friend of ours by the name of Dr. Jimmie Reed. In her book, *Who Me, Prophesy?* she wrote, "It really helps the everyday believer to understand that this channel is available to us to hear God and to understand God." As stated in 1 Corinthians 14:39-40, "Wherefore brethren, covet to prophesy and forbid not to speak with tongues, let all things be done decently in an order."

Prophesy is a channel used by God to communicate with us through spoken and written words, physical sensations, and heartfelt impressions. It is one of the gifts of the Holy Spirit that is listed in 1 Corinthians, chapter 12. It is an ability to speak for God under the inspiration of His Spirit in a known language. This is when a believer gets a glimpse into the heart of God. He or she may be quickened by the power of the Holy Spirit to understand the unknown and therefore, decode or convey knowledge in a known language to the receiver. Prophecy has been one of the communication channels through which many have been comforted, edified, and given divine directions for their lives.

The gift of prophecy can be a particular word for a specific time or a special need. It can either be written or spoken words, but it usually has a specific relatable meaning in your circumstance.

Tyndale Bible Dictionary defines prophecy with a group of Greek words. One of the linguistic variances of the word prophecy in Greek means to speak forth, proclaim or announce. However, in biblical Greek this term always carries the connotation of speaking, proclaiming, or announcing something under the influence of the Holy Spirit. Moreover, according to The Tyndale Dictionary, discernment is necessary because it is the wisdom to recognize truths from untruths by correctly evaluating whether a behavior or teaching is from God, human motivation, or the devil.

At some points in the past, I (Dr. Haupt) went up to a little mountain at Fort Totten in the Washington, DC area. I had told the Lord I was not going to mention her name or bring marriage up anymore. It was a settled deal for me, but a supernatural empowerment and an explosive prophetic announcement came up out of me and said, "GOD'S WOMAN." Then, I said, "Oh Lord, I said I was not going to mention it anymore." Operating in the prophetic reality of God's power usually overtakes the emotions or will of the individual. You speak the mind of God directly under the overwhelming presence of God. You are so inspired that you could not help but open your mouth to declare the heart and will of the Father. Hebrews 4:12 says, "For the Word that God speaks is alive and full of power [making it active, operative, energizing, and effective]; it is sharper than any two-edged sword, penetrating to the dividing line of the breath of life (soul) and spirit, and the [immortal] spirit, and of joints and marrow, [of the deepest parts of our nature], exposing *and* sifting *and* analyzing *and* judging the very thoughts and purposes of the heart."

However, the caution to be aware of with prophecy is that people tend to always seek out people with the gift. They want to be prophesied to. Prophecy is a channel of communication that has become extremely popular in church culture today. Therefore, prophecy requires us to be cautious because it can be misused by the immature of heart or carnal of mind. Prophecy is a valuable tool of faith but must also operate with love. God is the definition of love and the way in which believers use the gift prophecy should depict His loving nature.

CHAPTER FOURTEEN
CHANNEL 23
ENCOUNTERS AND VISITATIONS

There is an interesting story in the book of Judges 6:11-13 about Gideon, the son of Joash the Abiezrite. One day as he was threshing wheat in a winepress to hide it from the Midianites, the angel of the Lord came under the oak in Ophrah and began to speak to him about his position in the kingdom and the things he must do. Encounters like these are scattered across the Bible about men and women who experienced heavenly visitations and enjoy the attendant blessings. Remember, Abraham received three angels in Genesis 18. It was a glorious encounter for the faithful man. Not only was the mind of God revealed to him concerning Sodom and Gomorrah, his intercession and favor with God, saved his nephew, Lot, from the impending doom. Also, Abraham was able to unlock and obtain the fulfillment of the child of promise that had not manifested for many years. How about Jacob at Jabbok where he met God, and his name and destiny was changed and repurposed for good? According to Genesis 32: 22-31, clearly, that encounter set him on the right path for covenant blessings inherited by God's people currently, futuristically, and eternally.

Beloved, divine encounters are real. There are people who have encountered angels without even knowing. God wants you to be attentive to Him and He can do this by clothing Himself as a random stranger to talk to you. Although this is not a common channel of divine communication, it is still one of the means our God can choose to interact with us. Thus, it is just healthy to be attentive and receptive as you relate with others daily.

CHANNEL 24
SIGNS AND WONDERS

God also bearing them witness, both with signs and wonders, and with various miracles, and gifts of the Holy Spirit, according to His own will.
Hebrews 2:4 NKJV

By manifesting the supernatural, God affirms His authority and declares His sovereignty among men. He releases power and works miracles for the edification of the Church and the salvation of the lost. Jesus says in John 4:48 that unless people see signs and wonders, they will never believe. In other words, the demonstration of God's power is a statement of love and invitation for the lost and straying soul. Through signs and wonders, God confirms His ministers, builds up the faith of the Church and brings into the fold many who are still wandering the terrains of life in sin. It is beautiful to see the power of God in action, but you should never miss out of the message your heavenly Father is trying to communicate to you.

CHANNEL 25

NATURAL PHENOMENA

A natural phenomenon is an extraordinary occurrence or circumstance. Like many words with Greek roots, phenomenon started out as a science term. Scientists still use it to describe any event or facts that could be observed, amazing or not. It is to show, to shine, to appear, to be manifested, or to manifest itself. In John 12:27-30, Jesus said, "Now my soul is troubled. What shall I say, 'Father, save Me from this hour?' But for this purpose, I came to this hour. Father, glorify Your name." Then a voice came from heaven saying, "I have both glorified it and will glorify it again." Therefore, people who stood by and heard it said that it had thundered. Others said, "An angel has spoken to him." Jesus answered and said, the voice did not come because of me, but for your sake." That was a natural phenomenon. It was God speaking but they heard it as thunder.

Moses saw the burning bush, which is a common scene in the wilderness. The surprising observation of the fiery bush was that it burned but was not consumed. Also, a voice was coming out of the bush, calling Moses to his purpose in Egypt.

Today, God still makes himself known by nature. The voice of God can be revealed through mountains, water, trees, metals, and landscapes. God will do things in nature to confirm His reality.

CHANNEL 26
GOD SPEAKS THROUGH CIRCUMSTANCES

The Lord gave this message to Jonah son of Amittai: "Get up and go to the great city of Nineveh! Announce my judgment against it because I have seen how wicked its people are." But Jonah got up and went in the opposite direction to get away from the Lord. He went down to the seacoast, to the port of Joppa, where he found a ship leaving for Tarshish. He bought a ticket and went on board, hoping that by going away to the west, he could escape from the Lord. But... the Lord flung a powerful wind over the sea, causing a violent storm that threatened to send the ship to the bottom. Fearing for their lives, the desperate sailors shouted to their gods for help and threw cargo overboard ... Then he [Jonah] told them that he was running away from the Lord ... "Throw me into the sea," Jonah said, "and it will become calm again." ...Then the sailors picked Jonah up and threw him into the raging sea, and the storm stopped at once... Now the Lord had arranged for a great fish to swallow Jonah. And Jonah was inside the fish for three days and three nights.
Jonah 1: 1-5, 10, 12, 15, 17 NLT

God troubled the sea to tell Jonah to quit his aimless journey to Tarshish when souls were perishing in Nineveh. Prophet Jonah's disobedience caused trouble for himself and distress to others on the ship with him. Clearly, God was speaking through the tumultuous storm and Jonah understood exactly what He was saying. God uses some of the experiences we go through to tell us to grow up, become more patient, talk less, be more obedient, increase in faith, and so on.

Another example of God speaking through situations is when He caused the donkey of Balaam to stumble, intentionally declaring to the Prophet that he was heading the wrong way. And ultimately, to make His will clear, God literally caused Balak's donkey to speak (Numbers 22:26-34). There could be times in life when you really do not understand *why* and cannot figure your way out. That is the right time to turn to the Holy Spirit for understanding to know what God is saying through unfolding events. Sometimes our circumstances speak clearly to us. The Holy Spirit interprets our experiences and gives us a deeper understanding and clarity about those situations. As 1 Thessalonians 5:16-18 says, "Rejoice always, pray continually, give thanks in all circumstances, for this is God's will for you in Christ Jesus."

love of God by letting our light shine. For believers in the household of faith, God can use other people's experiences of growth and maturity to challenge us to pray and seek His presence more.

CHAPTER FIFTEEN
CHANNEL 27
GOVERNMENT AND AUTHORITIES

Let everyone be subject to the governing authorities, for there is no authority
except that which God has established. The authorities that exist have been
established by God. Consequently, whoever rebels against the authority is
rebelling against what God has instituted, and those who do so will bring
themselves to judgment.
Romans 13: 1-2 NIV

God raises and installs leaders to keep the world in order. He set them in authority to govern the affairs of the people, ensure peaceful coexistence, and encourage growth and development. Leadership is one of the earliest responsibilities of humans; an institution that attracts so much interest and attention of God. Without the government to ensure boundaries, enforce laws, and enhance growth, the earth will simply be in a state of chaos. Everyone will be free to do as they please, regardless of morals, and we will return to the primitive world where only the strongest survive.

After the fall of man written in Genesis 3, God knew that we would most likely destroy one another if He did not set some kind of authority in place to govern us. Nevertheless, we are not to worship the government but to obey its laws. It is not about political affiliation or personal interest. We are to respect, support, and continually pray for them because they are installed by God.

Leadership is not only in politics. If we start from the home, for example, we will see a structure in place that should be respected. The husband has a role and responsibility as the head and main provider of the family. Likewise, the wife has a leadership responsibility, and the children also have theirs. Failing to recognize these things and living in a family as you please will lead to conflict and sadly, in some cases, separation. Today, many households are headed by single women, who shoulder the responsibilities of rearing children, securing income, paying bills, managing the home environment, transportation, and much more. Hats off to them but they should not have to bear such a heavy leadership role and it appears to be a systemic situation. We may consider, how would God want us to help single mothers? Is He speaking to us, but we have turned a deaf ear? Remember, He speaks in both favorable and unfavorable circumstances.

Beyond family leadership, there are leaders in nations, communities, organizations, churches, groups, companies, agencies, and other entities. There are presidents, prime ministers, congresspersons, governors, mayors, commissioners, judges, city council and school board members, and many more types of leaders. God goes through leaders to make policies, enact laws, coordinate activities, disburse justice, expend resources, among other duties, for the good of everyone. This is why we should pray that our leaders are continually inspired by God not to be selfish and obsessed with power. Respect for leadership and those in authority is advocated in the Bible.

Therefore submit yourselves to every ordinance of man for the Lord's sake, whether to the king as supreme or to governors, as to those who are sent by him for punishment of evildoers and for the praise of those who do good. For this is the will of God that by doing good you may put to silence the ignorance of foolish men."
1 Peter 2:13-15

In other words, even if we have harsh and inconsiderate leaders, we should show respect, not to curse and condemn them because we know authority is given by God. He raises and disposes men at will for He holds the hearts of kings and lords in His hands. We should not be fault finders and when there is a need to correct something in government, we should not get violent and abusive but explore the limitless power of prayer. Then, act in accordance with the will and leading of the Holy Spirit.

There are elders in the family, Church, and groups as well. They should be honored and respected. If God has set a mentor, a counselor or a leader over your life, be ready to listen to God through them because many times God will go through those you respect and honor to ensure certain blessings and lessons in your life. 1 Peter 5:5 NKJV says, "Likewise you younger people, submit yourselves to your elders. Yes, all of you be submissive to one another, and be clothed with humility, for 'God resists the proud, but gives grace to the humble.'" God is not pleased with rebellious children who constantly frustrate their parents with reckless, nonchalant, and negative attitudes. This was made clear in Exodus 20:12 NKJV, when God said, "Honor your father and your mother, that your days may be long upon the land which the Lord your God is giving you." So, for anyone who wants to have a good and long life, honor and respect are not optional.

DR. DANIEL HAUPT AND DOROTHY DANIEL

CHANNEL 28
MEDIA (NEWS) AND HISTORICAL ACCOUNTS

We are living in the age of information. By some estimates the accumulation of knowledge doubles every 18 months. We have vast libraries of information at our fingertips. You can quickly access information using the internet, social media, apps, videos, and cable TV. At the heart of globalization, recent advances in technology, from the internet to satellite communication, are factors that allow virtually anyone to instantly see and hear happenings about other people anywhere on the planet. And we can do this by looking at the news on our phones or TVs, watching various YouTube channels, reading electronic and printed newspapers and magazines.

The Scripture also states that this Gospel of the kingdom will be preached to all the nations (Matthew 24: 14). Today, due to technological advancement, this is literally being fulfilled as the Gospel is proliferated throughout the globe via all these different mediums—the internet, social media, and satellite.

It is important to recognize that God will use media to activate our faith and move us into things He wants us to be, do and have. We need to be sensitive to God's speaking and revealing divine messages through media. Satan will also try to manipulate this media to deceive and derail many. He aims to get us to doubt and question what God is saying. He wants to create an impression or an interpretation of criticism for the message of God in the media. When Oral Roberts went on TV, there were many Christian pastors who said he was demonic. In their opinion, he would get on that "one-eyed demon" and talk about Jesus. "How dare him!" They wondered and questioned. What sacrilege! They never knew that was going to be a major channel through which God was going to save billions of people in the world.

Unfortunately, today congregations have pastors who are saying, "Don't use Facebook, don't use Twitter, and ignore Instagram." God is the original technologist, and He will use these mediums to spread the truth about the cross and the sacrifice of Christ for the salvation of the world. In spite of how Satan is abusing and misusing media for evil, God uses social media for good as a channel to speak *to* and *through* us to share the word of truth, help people, and advance His kingdom.

CHANNEL 29
ARTISTIC EXPRESSIONS AND DEMONSTRATIONS

The first covenant God made with His chosen people, the Hebrews, had regulations for worship and an earthly sanctuary. A tabernacle was set up in its first room where the lamp stood and the table with the consecrated bread. This was called the Holy place. Behind the second curtain was a room called the most Holy place, which had the golden altar of incense and the gold covered Ark of the Covenant. This Ark contained a gold jar of manna, Aaron's staff, and the stone tablets of the covenant. Above the Ark was the structure of two Cherubim of the glory overshadowing the cover. We cannot expound on the intricate details now, but all these pieces of art had great spiritual significance. They represented truth, patterns, ideas, and how things work. In fact, I (Dr. Haupt) use the tabernacle design even in my prayer life. When approaching God, I come to Him through the gates with praise, acknowledging who He is. I decree His redemptive power of holy names and the purposes He represents. I go to the brazen altar and confess my sins. Now that He's allowing me into the gate, the closer I get to him, the more unholy I can feel because I recognize the difference between His standards and mine. And so, all the pieces of furniture had not only artistic expression, but prophetic truth and meaning that speak to the people of God, even today.

Art, dance, music, imagery, pottery, and other creative works can be used as a vehicle for God to communicate. In the story of the Potter and the clay, the prophet went down to the Potter's house to see something. What we go and see on the Potter's wheel can speak to us by the Spirit of God. So, art is very important because it has the power to speak a rhema word of God to us today.

In first Chronicles 15:16, David commanded the chief of the Levites to appoint their brothers as the singers and musicians who would play loudly on harps, cymbals, and other musical instruments to minister sounds of joy. David himself had mastered the art of music and poetry. Also, poetic artistry is in the book of the Songs of Solomon.

There are so many ways to behold art and recognize the messages it speaks. There are actual designs created by designers whose artistic work is so uniquely beautiful, people desire to buy their products. Hebrews 8:5 tells us that the tabernacle was a copy, shadow, and a pattern of the heavenly. Many times, through art expression, people convey heavenly thoughts, principles, and communications through their designs. Many people in the church may desire to be prophetic preachers. But if one could be a prophetic artist, he or she could change the world. A prophetic artist can present vision and truth so creatively. Every time you see a yellow M arch, what does that tell you? What does that depict? McDonald's! Seeing that M for McDonald's triggers a desire in many consumers to go and eat that fast food. God uses art the same way to put desires in us through anointed aesthetic appeal. So, art is a significant channel of communication that God uses to speak to us today

There are some religious movements that will not allow drums in the atmosphere. They refuse to allow any pictures to express people's thoughts. I (Dr. Haupt) chuckled while in Korea observing a picture of Jesus on the wall. That picture of Jesus had slanted eyes like Koreans. I recognize, we should be multicultural in our art expressions, especially when expressing the person of Jesus. People tend to express their feelings and ideas about God through their art form. This is a powerful area that needs to recognized as an authentic channel for God to speak to us.

CHANNEL 30
KINESTHETIC HANDS-ON DEMONSTRATION

Then I went down to the potter's house, and there he was making something at the wheel. And the vessel that he made of clay was marred in the hand of the potter; shaping from the clay was marred in his hands; so he made it again into another vessel, as it seemed good to the potter to make. Then the word of the LORD came to me saying: "O house of Israel, can I not do with you as this potter?" ...
Jeremiah 18:3-6a NKJV

Through the kinetic principle of the Potter's house, God can also connect with us. He led Jeremiah to the potter's house to observe him making a vessel with his hands. As Jeremiah watched, the word of God came to him speaking. The Kinetic channel is the process through which we connect with God as people observe people doing things with their hands. Our God is not limited and can devise any means to communicate His intentions with us. We must be watchful and ready to receive from Him, even from the demonstration of handicrafts.

CHANNEL 31
SCIENCE: INVESTIGATIVE EVIDENCE AND SYSTEMS (DNA), ASTRONOMY

*And God said, "Let there be lights in the vault of the sky to separate the day from the night, **and let them serve as signs to mark sacred times,** and days and years, and let them be lights in the vault of the sky to give light on the earth." And it was so. God made two great lights —the greater light to govern the day and the lesser light to govern the night. He also made the stars.*
Genesis 1: 14-16 NIV

The universe of matter, space and time is knitted with the mysteries of God verified by the scriptures and scientific evidence. With the help of science, we can unravel and harness some of these mysteries for our own good. The scripture above reveals that the stars, for example, are signs or markers of sacred times.

Astronomy is a scientific field instituted by God. We read in Psalm 147: 4 and in Isaiah 40:26 that the Lord called forth the starry host and determined the number of the stars. He called each one by name because of His great power and mighty strength. As countless as they are, the stars are named, numbered, and assigned with purpose by God. Specific names given to each of the stars are significant. Moreover, the scientific process of naming them was designed to reveal the events of Jesus' birth, life, resurrection, and return.

Marilyn Hickey, in her book , expounds on the truth and value of astronomy to point us toward our salvation in Jesus Christ and exposes Satan's lie about astrology. His lie is designed to keep us from understanding the way to salvation while worshipping the creature (created beings, matter, and cosmos) more than the Creator. In proper context, when our Creator is honored, astrology is a valid science. E.W. Bullinger in his book, *The Witness of the Stars*, displays how the constellations witness to the accuracy of biblical prophetic truths. He uses celestial charts and illustrations to back his conclusions. Michael O'Connell, in his book, *Finding God In Science*, helps us to discover God in science and explains the consistency of science within the Bible in plain language. We know from scripture that God is an organic scientist and inventor. Hebrews 11:3 outlines that He built the structure of the universe.

Scriptural evidence illustrates that Christ's earthly message aligns with the natural laws of the universe, and prophetically reveals a divine premeditation or intention in the earth's creation and ecosystem. We are spiritually, biologically, and culturally wired individually to commune with God. For instance, we all have different DNA, an abbreviation of deoxyribonucleic acid, which is the molecule that contains the genetic code of organisms. We grow up in different cultures, ethnic groups, creeds and colors. However, regardless of these cultural or biological differences, God wants to communicate with every one of us. He has created many channels to make this possible.

CHAPTER SIXTEEN

INSURANCE VS ASSURANCE

Insurance in financial jargon is a term that is used to refer to coverage of unforeseen circumstances surrounding an event, such as theft, fire, or flood. What we have in Christ is an assurance of life which is deeper than the promises of insurance. God says in Jeremiah 33: 3, "Call on me and I will answer you, and will tell you great and hidden things that you have not known." He also says in Jeremiah 29:11, "I know the plans I have for you, declares the Lord, plans for good and not of evil, to give you a future and a hope."

Hearing the voice of God is a part of the kingdom benefit package, especially for those who are spiritually covered. Christianity is not simply a religion but a religion but a relationship. Knowing God as Father and Friend is the essence of our spiritual adoption into His Family. We are sons and daughters of the Most High God. His ears are ever ready to listen when we pray, and His heart yearns for fellowship. What believers have is heaven on earth because we have the peace of God in our hearts and the abiding presence of God leading us each moment of the way.

God wants to speak to you. He has sent the Spirit of Truth to guide you into all truth and direct you every step of the way (John 16:13).

HEARING THE VOICE OF GOD IS A BIRTHRIGHT FOR THE SAINTS

Jesus paid the price for human redemption, providing access to all the heavenly technologies which includes hearing the voice of God in the earth. Just as Romans 8:14 puts it, "For all who are being led by the Spirit of God, these are the sons of God." Beloved in Christ, being a member of God's family qualifies you to hear God and have access to all the family resources. He says, "Call on Me and I will answer and show you great and unsearchable things you do not know" (Jeremiah 33:3 NIV). He also promised to "give you hidden treasures, riches stored in secret places" (Isaiah 45:3 NIV). He says in Jeremiah 29:12 (NIV), "You will call upon Me and come and pray to Me, and I will listen to you." It is not His will to be far from you. He wants to be your friend. He knows the darkness of time can be terrible, the days can be busy, and life can be tiring.

God wants to bear your burden and be your closest friend. Have you given Him a chance? It is not about being a Christian by birth. Are you born spiritually into the wonderful family of Christ? Is your heart renewed to be sensitive to His voice? Do not forget that His sheep know His voice and by default, they respond to Him. When He, the Great Shepherd of the sheep (saints) calls, they follow (John 10:27). You can simply invite Him to take charge of your life today if you have not done so. Ask Him to come into your heart and be your Lord. Then, wonderful journey of kingdom exploits begins.

HIS VOICE EMPOWERS US FOR KINGDOM PRODUCTIVITY

Hearing the voice of God empowers us to be God's operatives and collaborators in kingdom exploits on the earth. We are Christ ambassadors and God's representatives here (2 Corinthians 5: 20). "We are fellow workers with Christ who should not receive the grace of God in vain (2 Corinthians 6:1). God confides in those who love and fear Him and makes His covenant known to them (Psalm 25: 14). We all need one another to work in synergy for the glory of God. To be relevant in our generation and culture, we must be connected to Father and all His technologies in order to transform the world.

Daniel, a man who enjoyed divine communication, declares, "He [God] reveals the deep and hidden things; He knows what lies in darkness, and light dwells with Him" (Daniel 2:22). Daniel 11:32 (NKJV) summarizes it by saying "… the people who know their God shall be strong and carry out great exploits." Exploits are possible in the world when the Church is divinely connected.

HIS VOICE RELEASES MULTIDIMENSIONAL PERSPECTIVE

Discerning the voice of God is His method to release solutions through a multi-dimensional perspective for areas of life. In Isaiah 45:3 (NLT), God says, "I will give you the treasures of darkness and the hidden riches of secret places, so that you may know that I am the Lord…" What do you think would become of the world without inventors and pioneers who heard the voice of God? They were people who impacted the world, like Imhotep, first architect and physician in history; Sir Isaac Newton, astronomer and physicist of the universal gravitation theory; Samuel Morse, inventor of the telegraph, which sent signals called the Morse code; Harriet Tubman, abolitionist and activist, led over 300 slaves to freedom; Washington Carver, scientist and inventor of 300 products; Charles Drew, surgeon and researcher, created the storage and processing for blood transfusions; Katherine Johnson, aeronautics mathematician ("Hidden Figures"), provided calculations for space travel that enabled the first men to land on the moon; Michelangelo, world renowned artist, and so many others. But these innovators and many more lived a life of connection. They gave our world contributions that out lived them.

An excellent example of an inventor hearing the voice of God is George Washington Carver. He was able to discover the multi-functionality of the peanut because he fellowshipped with God. Carver's inquiries and God's answers are quite interesting.

George Washington Carver was a great scientist who often prayed and addressed God as "Mr. Creator." One night he walked out into the woods and prayed, "Mr. Creator, why did you make the universe?" He listened, and God said, "Little man, that question is too big for you. Try another." The next night he walked into the woods and prayed, "Mr. Creator, why did you make man?" He listened and God said, "Little man, that question is still too big for you. Try another."

The third night he went into the woods and prayed, "Mr. Creator, why did you make the peanut?" This is what he heard: "Little man, that question is just your size. You listen and I will teach you." And you know that George Washington Carver invented about three hundred ways to use the peanut.
-Excerpt from an OSOT article

This is what connection with God and hearing His voice can do through a life. "Eye have not seen, nor ear heard, nor have entered into the heart of man, the things which God has prepared for those who love Him" (1Corinthian 2:9). Many of us do not know how much we are loved by God. Growing in relationship with God will enable us to become a solution to our generation.

CHAPTER SEVENTEEN

RECOGNIZING GOD'S VOICE BEGINS WITH HIS WORD: LOGOS, RHEMA, AND DABAR

For the word of God is quick, and powerful, and sharper than any two-edged sword, piercing even to the dividing asunder of soul and spirit, and of the joints and marrow, and is a discerner of the thoughts and intents of the heart.
Hebrews 4:12 KJV

The word of God is the starting point to hearing and recognizing God's voice. In a busy world with several clashing doctrines proliferated among the people, it takes the students of the word to discern the voice of the Master from the noise and shout of the multitude. The Word of God is primary and central to His communication.

At the mature level, you should draw a distinction between the letters of the Scripture and the Person of the Scripture. Bible readers and students can misconstrue the scriptures with mere letters or words within the pages of the sacred book. However, the spiritual reality is that when you sit with the Word, you are actually at the feet of the Son of God. That is where the Holy Spirit opens and enlightens the eyes of our hearts to receive insight, inspiration, revelation, wisdom and instruction directly from heaven.

Hebrews 4:12 (NIT) makes it clear that the Word of God is living and powerful. John 1:1-5, 14 (NKJV) says:

In the beginning was the Word, and the Word was with God, and the Word was God. He was in the beginning with God. All things were made through Him, and without Him nothing was made that was made. In Him was life, and the life was the light of men. And the light shines in darkness, and the darkness did not comprehend it... And the Word became flesh and dwelt among us, and we beheld His glory, the glory was as of the only begotten of the Father, full of grace and truth.

As you can see from John 1, when talking about the word of God, we are referring to a Personality greater than mere letters and characters. The Bible is the tangible document of God's mysteries about the Person and ministry of Jesus; it is the greatest book ever written because it serves as our manual of understanding the incomprehensible God and all His wonderful promises. The Word of God is God and this Word is the Creator of all things. We read in Genesis 1 that God employed the agency of the Word in the creative process of the universe. He spoke things into existence. Everything seen in the observable universe was created by the active voice of God.

God the Spirit also resides in the redeemed; that is why we can say, "He that lives in us is greater than he that is in the world." The Trinity works as One and because God is One, the Word and the Spirit cannot contradict. The Holy Spirit does not speak as an independent Being and the Word cannot negate the verdict of the Holy Spirit because both are actually One—the unchanging God.

Beloved, we need to understand that communication with God is the primary source of divine communication. If you think you have received directions from God, check it with what the Word says. If it negates or contradicts, then you need to recheck and reverify before heading in that direction. Any other channel of communication is secondary. They are valid but become questionable if they contradict God's Word, for we know that our God is not the author of confusion.

God's Words come through the vehicle of Scriptures. This has been extensively explained under the Scripture Channel. The Word comes as logos (written word of God on general issues that serve as a measuring stick or standard of truth), Rhema (spoken or revealed word that can be personalized or applied to relevant situations), and Dabar (a pronounced action word pertaining to God's business at hand; it is the equivalent of the Greek words Logos and Rhema). The Word has become the primary channel of divine communication.

Consider why there are so many experiences of divine encounters in the Bible. In the days of the prophets, priests, judges, and kings in the Old and New Testaments, God spoke with thunder, lightning, fire, and an audible voice. The Bible says in Hebrews 1:1-2, "God, who at various times and in various ways spoke in time past to the fathers by the prophets, has in these last days spoken to us by His Son, whom He has appointed heir of all things, through whom also He made the world." We have said that Jesus is the Word personified and when you sit with the written word, you are actually at the feet of Jesus, God the Son. By the agency of the Holy Spirit, you will understand the heart and stance of God on general issues, get personal revelations or opened mysteries that can be applied to your life or situations around you.

Being a student and handler of God's Word is a prerequisite for capturing creative and life changing words from God. By consistently handling Scriptures, studying the 66 books of the Bible, meditating on the laws and precepts contained therein, audibly confessing and memorizing the verses, and positioning ourselves to hear with all readiness, inevitably stimulates communication between us and God. Much of God's Communication with the saints, especially the Word-disciplined disciples, happens on the basic level of thoughts. This has been recognized to be a spontaneous flow of thoughts, ideas, words, feelings, or pictures. As you continue to sit with the Word of God, communication between you and God becomes easier and smoother. This allows the Holy Spirit to inspire your heart with the thoughts and feelings of God which will make it obvious that God is speaking to you. His voice, even in our thoughts and feelings, is unmistakable. We recognize it because we know how divine and incomprehensibly clear He sounds. You need to make a decision today to be a lover and a student of the Word if you want to discern or recognize God's voice.

CHAPTER EIGHTEEN

RELATIONSHIP WITH GOD DETERMINES EVERYTHING

I t all begins and ends with a relationship. All the channels of divine communication mentioned in the previous chapters are within the benefits package of the birthrights of the believer. The children of the King of kings are not meant to go through life without the divine guidance of the Spirit.

Dear reader, God wants to speak to you, too. He has never limited His words to the prophets and priests of old. You have a place in the Kingdom, a purpose to fulfill on earth, and a position of fellowship and worship in eternity. It does not matter how many tears you have cried or how many fears are in your heart. His thought towards you are always thoughts of peace and not of evil, to give you a hope and a future (Jeremiah 29: 11).

You are loved and precious to the Creator and Sustainer of the universe. It is impossible to comprehend the depth, heights, breadth, and length of His love. It is eternally un-aging, outnumbers every grain of sand on earth, and is unconditional. He sees your burden and He is willing to lift it off your shoulders. He knows your struggles and He is willing to calm the storm for your sail. He understands your passion and desires to inspire you into the reality of your destiny.

God wants to whisper His love in your ears, inspire your heart with His wisdom, enlighten your eyes to see which way to go, and lead you by His consistent counsel to the *other side of through*. Have you given Him the chance and privilege to do that? Have you invited God to take His rightful place in your heart?

He needs your permission to order your steps. Yes, He is God unlimited in power and unstoppable in His sovereign might. Yet, out of His eternal wisdom, He has given you the right and freewill to choose whom to serve and worship. He will not interfere in your affairs freely unless you give Him the right and permission to do so. Will you allow God's reign to begin today, so you can start to enjoy the different dimensions of His promises? God can speak to anyone but His communion with the Christ-redeemed, blood-washed saints is seamless, unbroken, and everlasting. He communicates expressly with His own and His voice grows more audibly and unique through consistent usage.

We know these are perilous times and the world is gradually becoming more hostile because of satanic and human rebellion. We see it in the news, on TV and social media, and read it in publications. However, there is a huge difference between seeking peace on the battlefield of planet earth and having incredible internal peace amidst all the conflicts and crises of life. The peace and security we have is that which no human government can promise or give. How sweet to know that past sins are forgiven, the present is being ordered by God, and the future is secured in His arms.

Beloved, this is time to position yourself for divine connection to condition your heart for elevation and fulfill your destiny. Time is fleeting, the clock is ticking, and you need to be intentional about your fellowship with God. You do not have to make all the decisions of life by your own intellect; it is wise to know the will of God. The Bible says, "Trust in the LORD with all your heart, and lean not on your own understanding; in all your ways acknowledge Him, and He shall direct your paths. Do not be wise in your own eyes; fear the LORD and depart from evil. It will be health to your flesh and strength to your bones" (Proverbs 3: 5-8 NKJV).

You can invite God to intervene in your affairs now. "Because if you confess with your mouth that Jesus is Lord and believe in your heart that God raised Him from the dead, you will be saved. For with the heart one believes and is justified, and with the mouth one confesses and is saved. For everyone who believes in Him will not be put to shame. For there is no distinction between Jew and Greek; for the same Lord is Lord of all, bestowing His riches on all who call on Him. For everyone who calls on the name of the Lord will be saved" (Romans 10: 9-13).

More than you can imagine, God is willing to listen and speak to you. You are created for fellowship. Will you bow your head this moment and pray the following prayer?

Dear Lord Jesus,

You have opened my eyes to see that I am loved and created for intimate connection with You. I am not meant to walk my days on earth without Your guiding counsel each step of the way. I acknowledge that I have had difficulties in recognizing Your voice all these years and I am grateful for the revelation that You can speak to me in many unique ways. I ask O Lord, that You forgive me all the sins that are barricading an express flow of Your words and inspiration in me. Give me the grace to be positioned to receive from You. Help me to filter Your voice from the noise and distractions of the world. Grant me that discerning spirit to know and understand You each time You speak to me. I want my ears to be opened and my heart to become sensitive to pick spiritual signals from You. Make me a lover of Your word and take away the veil obscuring Your will concerning my life. I receive the power and grace to walk in the reality of divine fellowship with You. I decree that from this moment on, I am connected to You. May I no longer struggle to hear Your voice and receive from You. Thank you, Lord because I know You have sent gracious answers to my prayers. In Jesus name I have prayed. Amen.

CITATIONS AND RECOMMENDED READINGS

Comfort, P. W., & Elwell, W. A. (Eds.), (2001). *Tyndale Bible Dictionary.* Carol Stream: Tyndale House Publishers, Inc.

Foter, G. (1988). *The Purpose and Use of Prophecy: A New Testament Perspective.* Dubuque: Kendall/Hunt Publishing Company.

Hagin, K. E. (1987). *Concerning Spiritual Gifts: 26 Lessons on The Holy Spirit and His Gifts.* Tulsa: Kenneth Hagin Minstries, Inc.

Hamon, B. (2004). *Student Workbook for Manual for Ministering Spiritual Gifts.* Sana Rosa Beach: Christian International Ministries Network.

Haupt, D. (Ed.). (2019). *Destiny: The Other Side of Through.* Arvada: Danmil Publishing.

Hayden, S. (2001). *Until Christ is Formed.* Sandra Hayden.

Hickey, M. (2015). *Signs in the Heavens.* Greenwood Villiage: Marilyn Hickey Ministries.

O'Connell, M. (2016). *Finding God In Science: Extraordinary Evidence for the Soul and Christianity, a Rocket Scientist's Gripping Odyssey Non-Illustrated Version.* Orange County: Eigen Publishing.

Price, P. A. (1984). *The Prophet's Dictionary: The Ultimate Guide to Supernatural Wisdom.* New Kensington: Whitaker House.

Rath, T. (2007). *Strengths Finder 2.0.* New York: Gallup Press.

Reed, J. (2004). *Who Me, Prophesy?* Xulon Press.

Stanley, C. (1985). *How to Listen to God.* Nashville: Thomas Nelson, Inc.

Virkler, K., & Virkler, M. (2013). *4 Keys to Hearing God's Voice: Teen Edition.* Lamad Publishing.

Virkler, M., & Virkler, P. (2010). *4 Keys to Hearing God's Voice.* Shippensburg: Destiny Image Publishers, Inc.

Dr. Daniel Haupt is an educator, social entrepreneur, and founder of the Destiny Center, a research and training enrichment epicenter. He is a prophetic seer and "Kingdomcentric" Bible teacher who hosts the international "Voice of Destiny Show" and the "Model Ant Podcast and Master Classes" with the Destiny Center. He is recognized internationally as an anthologist author, life coach, and leadership mentor.

Dr. Haupt is a destiny thought leader with a vision for helping emerging leaders to discover their purpose and act on their dreams(destiny). His heartfelt mission is to equip people to *be*, *do*, and *have* all God has destined for them by providing training for the discovery of personal and professional destiny priorities and models to fulfill God-given potential.

Dr. Haupt has a B.S. in Organizational Management, an MBA in Corporate Training, and a D. Min in Church Leadership. He is currently matriculating an ED in Organizational Leadership at Grand Canyon University, Phoenix, Arizona.

He and his wife of 32 plus years, Millicent, and their six young adult sons and daughters, Daniel (DJ), Imani, Michael, Danae, Destiny, and James reside mostly in the Denver, Colorado and Washington, DC metropolitan areas.

DESTINY COMMUNITY DEVELOPMENT CENTER

The Destiny Center is a research and training enrichment epicenter for the seven mountains of influence (priesthood, human development, government, education, communication, entertainment, and economics); a vision to empower an emerging generation of innovators and catalysts to *be*, *do* and *have* everything God has destined for them. The Destiny Center is the home of the Model Ant Podcast and Master Classes.

Dr. Daniel Haupt, Founder & Director

www.destinycommunitycenter.org

Email: drhaupt@destinycommunitycenter.org

Danmil Travel

For Information

on Travel Services

visit www.danmiltravel.com

To register for upcoming destination events and encounters like our Summer Cruise or Christmas in Africa adventure, email: info@danmiltravel.com

---

Prophet Dorothy Daniel is the overseer of The Gift of Love Ministry, along with her husband of 48 years, Edmund Daniel Sr. She is a gifted prophetic teacher, human developer, and mentor. Hearing the Voice of God is her specialty in ministry. Her purpose is to teach and encourage God's people, so they are equipped and mobilized to live victoriously during these challenging times.

Prophet Daniel is recognized globally as a leader to leaders like Prophet Deborah in the Old Testament. She has a Certificate of Completion from CI of the Rockies, School of Prophets. She is ordained by Pastors Gregory and Sherly Burns of Spoken Word Ministries and Dr. Jimmie Reed, Overseer of Revolution Global Center. Currently, she serves at Faith4Life Church in Round Rock, Texas, under Pastors Evan and Pricilla Black. Also, she serves as a Consultant and Prophet for My Father's House Church in Fort Worth, Texas, under the administration of Pastor Harriet Reed.

After many years of service as an educator, she retired from Kipp Austin Public Schools as a Special Education Associate. There she worked with at-risk students as part of Kipp Arts and Letters Academy College Prep.

She and her husband, Edmund, reside in in Hutto, Texas. They have two sons, Edmund II and Carlos, three grandchildren, Michael, Na'Shyra, and Isaiah, and one great grandchild, Malachi Daniel.

Where love reigns, let love rule your life.

The Gift of Love Ministry is a charity that is here because of the love they have for God and His people. God put a yearning in our hearts to share His principles with others for developing moral values that enhance character as well as help with other relationships.

Prophet Dorothy Daniel, overseer

www.tgolm.net

dorothytgolm@aol.com

Instagram: @thegiftofloveministry

Destiny: The Other Side of Through

An Anthology

by Dr. Daniel Haupt, Danette Padilla, Derrick Haynes, Destiny Haupt, Dorothy Daniel, Ella Coleman, Juanita Harris, Katrina Ferguson, Lanora Witherspoon, Paul Thornton, Dr. Sandra Hayden, Shaw Barkat, Shelley Fisher, S. Danette Padilla, Dr. Vivian Moore, Dr. Jimmie Reed

"Destiny: The Other Side of Through" can help you discover powerful secrets to managing what appears to be reroutes to your destiny that are actual opportunities disguised as crises. The stories and teachings in this anthology will inspire you to recognize your true north, your place and position of optimal purpose and effective functioning. This work is designed to empower you to act on the dreams God has given you—to be, do and have what He has always destined for you. This book will remind you of the most important truth you can discover about yourself is that you are a Designer original, endowed with purpose and destiny which inspired God to create you. Despite the circumstances in which you were born, or the life battles you must fight, the best version of yourself is still emerging. The Lord is testing your character like He did Joseph's in the Bible, until the time came to fulfill his dreams (Psalm 105:19). "Destiny: The Other Side of Through" is a synergistic work of writers inspired to scribe an anthology about purpose and destiny. It is an integrated, Kingdom of God, principle-centered approach to thriving in your journey on the road to destiny.

ISBN: 978-1-7342003-0-0 Paperback 154 pages

Soon to be published:

Raising Your Destiny Flags: Discover How You are S.H.A.P.E.D.

by Dr. Daniel Haupt

When it comes to pursuing our purpose and destiny, people often ask several vital questions: Why were we born? What is our calling? What is our purpose? What is our assignment while here on the earth? What individual contributions can we make to cause our communities to become a better place? How do we use our God-given gifts and talents to become uniquely successful during our lifetime? These are important questions that must be answered if people are going to fulfill their dreams, implement their visions, and maintain a sense of accomplishment. Dr. Haupt addresses these questions in this book.

ISBN: 978-1-7342003-2-4   Paperback